Becoming Sar'h:

A Modern Self-Realization Story

Lauren Hutton

PRAISE FOR BOOK ONE

"A Master's Story in Her Own Words…I too could not put the book down."

"Lauren's book is an eloquently written, authentically told true story of her journey through awakening into mastery. The book is filled with deep wisdom, vividly narrated experiences, and many surprising twists. If you are curious about the bridge between spiritual mysteries and real life, read the book and you'll find yourself walking that bridge. I particularly enjoyed the multidimensional nature of the book, and the Self-love that could be heard in the narrator's voice. A book that opens the mind and the heart alike, it is a gem for anybody choosing the path of enlightenment."

"This story weaves you in and out of imagination, tragedy, and the golden nuggets of wisdom that are discovered as one oscillates between the human and the soul. Just as if you were listening to a dear friend, Lauren shares her perspective directly, with no bull. This straight talk is valuable for those going through the awakening experience, in that it busts up some of the common expectations of enlightenment, and shows a real picture of what it looks like. It provides comfort to those that might feel alone in their journey and serves as an inspiration to others to share the incredible experience of falling apart and letting the light in."

"My new favorite author! A page-turner, a delightful journey into an expanded view of SELF – Lauren's story resonates at a soul level with a narrative that is widely infused with magic. A must read for those who have chosen to take the road less travelled."

"This book is definitely not for everyone, it is going to transform and shift something in you. It will not leave you unchanged."

"Inspiring and honest. I love this book."

"I wasn't expecting the need to devour the book in one sitting when I purchased it. But that is exactly what I did. I simply couldn't put it down once I'd started reading Lauren's story. Becoming Sar'h is an honest telling of one woman's search for her true Self. Lauren does a sterling job of keeping the story flowing, all the while allowing Sar'h to introduce great wisdom throughout. Fair warning. Like a real pro, Lauren has ended Book One on a cliffhanger! Which leaves me anxiously waiting for Book Two!"

BECOMING SAR'H

CONTENTS

CONTENTS

"So was I once myself a swinger of birches.
And so I dream of going back to be...
I'd like to get away from earth awhile
And then come back to it and begin over.
May no fate willfully misunderstand me
And half grant what I wish and snatch me away
Not to return. Earth's the right place for love:
I don't know where it's likely to go better.
I'd like to go by climbing a birch tree,
And climb black branches up a snow-white trunk
Toward heaven, till the tree could bear no more,
But dipped its top and set me down again.
That would be good both going and coming back.
One could do worse than be a swinger of birches."

—Robert Frost, Birches

This book is dedicated to my dog,

Professor Ollie,

and to Robert Frost

—one could certainly do worse.

DISCLAIMERS

The offerings found here are for those who have moved beyond awakening and spiritual dabbling, and dive directly into the dark night of the soul, realization while staying in physical form, and what comes after.

If you are looking to improve your human life, please do not read this book. If you are looking to gain spiritual 'powers', please do not read this book. If you are looking for answers outside of yourself without a strong understanding of your own internal wisdom, please do not read this book.

Before reading or consuming any consciousness-opening material, it is always a good idea to ask yourself, is this the highest and best information for me at this time?

These offerings discuss matters in depth that could potentially derail and slow down the perfection of the soul evolution occurring naturally within you. If you open to the senses of the soul and attempt to cross the threshold into your realization prematurely, the effects can be quite disastrous.

The information contained herein is only the author's personal experiences. In the event that you use the information contained in this book for yourself, the author and publisher do not assume responsibility for your actions or outcomes.

This is your journey, and you are responsible for all the creations in your life.

Should you need medical or mental health support, please seek the advice of a licensed professional in your area.

Names and places have been left out of the book or changed to protect the privacy of those involved.

ACKNOWLEDGEMENTS

I want to personally thank Karen Falk for her continuous role of wisdom librarian and for her unwavering support of all my writing, from the beginning. Additionally, she helped me move these experiences to paper, in a way for conscious readers to understand, and I am beyond grateful for her questions, feedback, and willingness to dive into whatever I shared. I am forever grateful for your friendship, Karen.

In addition, I thank Maureen Supeene, Sylvia Konrad, and Sarah Seymour for reading and providing feedback on parts and pieces of this book. I thank all those who gathered under the Banyan Tree in the space formerly called the Center of Being. This is not only my story, but one you all helped write on the halls of humanity as well.

Thank you to patrons who supported this publication and all of my writing, with more than just their money. I'm looking at you, Sue, Joyce, Ruth, and Momo.

Finally, a big thank you to the 'sovie amigas' for being there to greet me when I crossed the threshold into a sovereign state of being.

I love you all — deeply, completely, and freely.

LETTER TO THE READER

Dear friends and readers,

Welcome to the web of consciousness I spun into the next volume of the *Becoming Sar'h* book series. I hope you enjoy dancing with me in the cobwebs of creation.

For new readers, *Becoming Sar'h* is the story of the grandest love affair you can have—the one with Self[1]. From the age of four, a voice I call Sar'h (pronounced sa-RA) played a major role in my life. This voice held wisdom far beyond my childhood years and served as an unwavering pillar of truth in a world driven by the whims of the collective human consciousness.

Sar'h is the voice of my soul or over soul[2] and has experienced many incarnations on Earth—lives filled with magic and meaning and lives filled with darkness and destruction.

Later I remembered this current human incarnation of Self, Lauren, was simply a physical and earthly expression of my soul, but not before I got completely lost in the singular human experience and later in the experience of the spiritual collective consciousness.

The *Becoming Sar'h* book series is the story of me, Lauren, the extremely

---

[1] I use Self, with a capital S, to refer to the totality of who I am, the multiple nature of Self, including my soul, physical human attributes, the I Exist, and wisdom distilled from all lifetimes, realities, and experiences as one.

[2] Soul — Individualized Spirit — refers to the immortal, immaterial essence of my being and holds all the wisdom distilled from every lifetime and experiences on Earth and outside of it. The soul has no birth and no death. It exists beyond time, duality, linearity, and physical expression. The over soul encompasses all human expressions of all lifetimes on Earth and in between.

imperfect human expression of Self, reconciling, sometimes extremely reluctantly, with the wise voice within—that of Sar'h. The first book I published in 2017 and here again in updated form covered my awakening into the true nature of who I am and what it means to be on planet Earth in from within an expanded view.

In this book, I do just about everything to get rid of, or bury my soul voice in order to fit into the modern world—antidepressants, drugs, and worst of all, developing an addiction to external success—the modern version of the plague sweeping across our increasingly technocratic[3] world. However, in this plague, bodies aren't buried in mass graves, souls are— rapidly and easily discarded for a false promised land of wealth, health, and happiness just as fleeting as the short time our bodies live on Earth.

It took the death of my father to shake me out of the illusion the physical world in front of me was all there was to know and a dear friend of lifetimes and beyond named El Morya to light the way when I got too lost in the dark to carry on alone.

In the end, I was never alone, but the perception can be palpable on this journey to end the cycle of reincarnation and step into the realized state of being. Once I remembered who I was from the experience and expanse of the soul, Sar'h and I traveled the world on one of the grandest adventures imaginable, as my human self, Lauren, faced her biggest fears—death of all identity and the extremities of aloneness.

By Book Two, I realize my human desire to be externally perceived as successful was actually a case of mistaken identity. What I really wanted to experience, above all experiences available, was self-realization and to document my shift in awareness in the written word for anyone choosing consciousness over automation[4] for eons to come.

---

[3] Technocratic in this context is characterized by the control of society by technology. This is also a reference to the automation of Earth, in which sweeping technological advances in artificial intelligence (AI) develop in tandem, or in mimic of, the collective consciousness of Earth. The more people choose soul-based consciousness over technological automation and a mind-based singular life; the more the AI will reflect that, which has severe and important consequences for the future of this planet.

[4] Choosing consciousness over automation is a reference to the importance of why many beings are choosing to self-realize at this significant time on Earth. With the development of AI, and in our increasingly technocratic world, in which technology becomes the new God of the collective belief systems of humanity, anyone choosing to live a multi-conscious, multi-reality existence, for themselves, in turn, impact on the evolution of Earth and humanity as a collective.

Even though I was not born to become a wise man on the mountain top or into a preordained spiritual family or any kind of special sacred life, I knew from a young age realization was mine to claim in this life. Even if I was a chubby kid, growing up in suburban Houston, I knew from the age of four this life was going to be it.

In growing up with this knowing of what was to come, I also knew I held deep desire to share my story. Not at all grand or holy, the path leading to my personal self-realization was messy, chaotic, and brought me to my knees over and over and over again, before I found the state of constant and consistent consciousness I enjoy today.

I want anyone who ever doubts realization is available to them to know—if you choose, you can live a life of freedom and experience a new way of living, along with thousands of others, as we write the book on what it means to live as a modern master of Self in the New Energy[5].

I started piecing together Book Two while crashing at my mother's condominium in Rockport, Texas in the fall of 2018. Hit by Hurricane Harvey in August the previous year, the condominium complex was a mess of rubble and debris, making it uninhabitable for most of its former residents.

My mother's place remained untouched by the storm, like a little pocket of light in a dark, dark world. Previously, I tried to escape to a forest retreat to write, but the silence which fell over the post-apocalyptic scene there worked too. As I wrote, the tarps covering the shattered windows from Harvey flapped heavily in rainy coastal winds. Not a voice or a thought could be heard below the swoosh of the wind as I was one of a small handful of people braving the post-storm scenario.

Coming through my own self-realization a few months after the storm, which inflicted $125 billion in damage and killed at least seventy people, I deleted my Facebook account thinking, "What is the need for such a thing in the realization experience?"

Then I remembered, "Oh yeah. I have a story to tell and to get out to those choosing the same." Increasingly, I find I relate more to Forrest Gump than any other character in my realized state of being. Everything is simple and in the moment. I do not store knowledge anymore, it's all

---

[5] New Energy is what comes after the New Age. This evolution of energetic dynamics allows the integration of duality, supremely the human and divine parts of Self merging as one, becoming the singularly multiple, I Am. While the New Age was based on vibration and frequency, New Energy expands in all directions, from Self and in support of Self, without trying to change anything and honoring every person, situation, including the world's state of affairs, exactly where it is in any given moment. The paradox is through allowing this shift at the individual level, without trying to change the external, the individual's shift in expanded awareness has major implications for the evolution of Earth and humanity.

sensations instead.

In realization, I completely stripped off my human suit, my human identity, my human role on Earth. And, I left it off for a while. Shocked, I found myself still in physical form some months later—I really didn't know if I would wake up each morning at first—I decided to put my human suit back on, yet this time as an experience—as an act of consciousness—never mistaking this human meat suit for my limited identity ever again.

Although my human suit fit and looked a little different than before, I quickly adjusted. Like pulling a pair of stretchy jeans from the clothes dryer, I did some squats to stretch out the seat of the suit too, to create a little more room for movement.

As I got back onto the social media forum, it asked for my bio. I cheekily wrote, "Homeless realized being traveling the world in a bikini and sweatpants." It was true, yet I quickly hit the backspace button, watching the characters on the screen disappear.

I knew many would not get the absurdity meant to be funny and even more would find it offensive. Once realized, you were never supposed to say it out loud or talk about it. In fact, I think most people expected you to do one of three things—go on with life pretending nothing ever happened, move to a mountain top and play hermit, or my favorite, throw on a white robe and run an ashram or something. What nonsense.

In the bio box, I replaced the words with lyrics from a John Lennon song, "I'm just sitting here watching the wheels go round and round. I really love to watch them roll. No longer riding on the merry-go-round I just had to let it go."

The beauty of vagueness. Sometimes that is all you can muster and share in this state of being. Everything else is taken too literally and always seems to run through the local linear loop of the human thought process, which nine times out of ten includes mind-based criticism rather than soul discernment.

This was not the first lifetime I have—as a soul—experienced realization or enlightenment or whatever term is *en vogue* these days. Yet, it is Lauren's— as my human expression—first time to experience this beyond natural state of being, so why not write it this way. I could write about the other and make myself sound so ancient and wise and more so, authoritative—and sell more books—but the current truth is those ancient stories are no longer relevant.

In the self-realized state of being, I find I am no longer operating in the past-present-future model, only this now experience, which sounds unbelievably and eye-rollingly cliché. But hey, that's where I find myself: here and here and here—in the infinitely multiple yet singularly now moment.

Further, I sense deeply, a record number of souled beings in physical human form moving from the initial awakening experience into the mastery of Self, and they are choosing to stay in physical form afterwards like me.

What I really want to explore are following questions: What in the world does that look like? And why do so many feel compelled to stay in physical form? What remains left to experience on Earth once you realize Earth is a stage and the human is playing a character, and you can't get lost in the play that is human life anymore? But before I can get you there, I have to take you through. I'm glad you are here, dear reader. Perhaps you won't learn anything new but instead see this story as a song where the lyrics may be different, but the tune is the same.

In honor of you and your unique journey,

Lauren and Sar'h as One

ADDITIONAL NOTES

Throughout the books I personify Sar'h's voice. It must be noted this is a writing tactic designed to bring the reader along on a journey. Indeed the soul does not speak with words, but rather in sensations, or feelings beyond the five human senses, which I have included for the sophisticated reader between the words. Not everyone's soul has a name, but we needed one here to tell a story.

To place words on an experience in which there is no set vocabulary and where no words will do justice is a daunting task, yet I have never shied away from such a task. Some will say this whole book is rubbish, and I cannot write. That's okay. They simply do not understand the multiple nature of this beautiful experience that is the 'last lifetime' on Earth—one ending the reincarnation cycle and in which all parts and pieces of Self from every lifetime and in between return to the home that is the sovereign Self.

Instead this is the book I wanted to read in the years between awakening and realization. For those just tuning into my writing, Sar'h represents my divinity and Lauren, my humanity, my human expression in physical form. The conversations between the two—between the human and the soul—represent the perceived struggle occurring between human will and divine will when moving from a spiritual awakening into the self-realization experience.

As the two voices emerge as one, so does the will, which becomes—in my unique experience—a singularly multiple, passion-less passion for soul expression and experience. I know that's a lot to say without saying it. Let me try again.

Eventually, I realized it was not about human will, or what the human wanted to experience, versus divine will, or what the soul sought to express, but a mode of operation in which the wills, or drive to experience and express merge as one.

The Return to Self—or self-realization as it is called these days—is also the end of suffering, for problems can no longer be perceived as problems and wounds can no longer be perceived as wounds. In other words, you cannot go back to playing your part in the human play, while forgetting it's just a play—an act of expression, for an experience. You always know it is a play, and you never forget you are on the Earth's stage.

Further, the dualistic battle of what it means to be both human and divine reconciles itself, while relaxing into the natural state of no separation, which is the Return to Self. In this state of being, the end of suffering does not mean everything is perfect and you never leave your wallet on a bus; you simply will not dive into the drama of having left your wallet on the bus. Instead, it becomes almost funny as you realize how you go about allowing your wallet to return to you—for a small and recent example.

Thus, what I am stating, is leading up to my realization in the book, I am writing in the experience of being not yet realized. I am writing from the perspective that the human and soul are separate. I am writing from the perspective wounds and problems still exist.

In Book Two, eventually the two voices—Lauren and Sar'h—merge with the I Exist, and become one voice, yet I do not portray it in my writing until it actually occurred for me, for self-realization was defined by the deep, soul-seated awareness that the two voices were never really separate but one all along.

Further, when the call to enlightenment, to self-realization, lights a fire within your soul, it is the most natural thing in all of human existence, and one of the paradoxes presenting itself is—it is when you feel the most alone and ostracized from family, society, and even spiritual or consciousness-related groups.

We are never alone, and I hope this book reminds others when they hit the bottom of the well, which is the sensation of 'alone' or loneliness, for this is the most alone the human, or ego, can ever feel.

It is my understanding self-realization cannot be taught in a classroom, a mystery school, a YouTube video, or an online class. In fact, the I Exist and the body of wisdom flowing from your soul is the only thing responsible for your realization.

And, on the other side of the coin, the magical part is sometimes you'll hear, read, or find yourself in the exact experience taking you further, bringing your human awareness in alignment with your expanded soul understanding. Perhaps a sentence or two in this book will do that for you.

Realization cannot be forced or manipulated by the human desire to be better, to become a perfect spiritual human being—there is no such thing! In fact, it only occurs in allowing the human expression to be itself fully—perfectly imperfect. Perfection is not a human condition—no matter how spiritual you project yourself to be externally. I still spill coffee all over myself most mornings, and sometimes I even yell. Realization has nothing to do with perfection, and in the end, zero to deal with spirituality.

When the passionate fire to know and be yourself ignites, everything you thought you knew as a human being, all your beliefs about right and wrong, any limitations of perceived duality and linearity will be incinerated before you cross the threshold into your realized state—including everything you picked up in the spiritual world. And it's a great thing, for you do not want to bring any limitations with you into the embodied enlightenment experience.

I said I was ready many times, but truly could not fathom all that burned. Even now, I find something will pop up—a belief system, a concept of what is right and wrong—yet before I can even examine it, there it is—glowing in the flames of awareness—automatically, and without effort. I find it best to let my human expression take a seat and warm its hands on the fire in the desert of my own consciousness.

El Morya and I define being[6] as a perpetual state of becoming—a never static, always dynamic experience of knowing yourself as God, too— also something I will cover in great detail.

In a state of perpetual becoming, writing something down on paper for people to read years later is a funny thing—especially in the context of the ever-changing tides of my own consciousness. As soon as I write something down, a gateway to a deeper awareness rolls in, and I sink deeper, leaning back into it, and the words become obsolete almost instantly.

I have made a perception shift in knowing I am simply capturing a moment. I can swallow this truth pretty easily because of my past as a newspaper reporter, in which I knew the days after I published an article it would be lining a kitty litter box pretty quickly. I'm happy to capture a moment and have it dissolve in a litter box the next day.

Just as I am willing to know what I write has a limited shelf life, I hope you too allow the ease and grace of discarding long-held beliefs, which once served but no longer do. The snake never stops shedding its skin. In the end, self-realization is a belief system-free state, in which everything is true and nothing is true. It's all just an experience or expression with a quick, sometimes immediate, expiration date. Cheers to letting it all go as easily as it came!

Through my writing practice, I am reminded of the impermanence of everything. After all, in a state of being, there is no end and no beginning to

---

[6] Being is state of perpetual becoming of Self, always dynamic, never static; a constant state of motion, requiring no physical movement. The dynamic perpetual becoming of Self occurs outside of linear time and physical space, yet in embodiment this experience extends to physical time and space.

our inimitable soul stories beyond the veils of maya.[7] In other words, there is no birth of the soul, nor is there ever an ending to the story. Once you incarnate on Earth, you can never go home, or back to where you came from. Instead, home becomes Self.

It is not until I reach the end of this book that I am able to fully express my soul's passion in a living breathing body—free from stories, identities, and beyond the illusion of maya. Yet any and all barriers holding anything separate had to come down before I could become all that I am in human form—embodiment. And, it wasn't until then that I could fully realize why I desired the experience from the depths of my soul so deeply I willingly gave up everything—absolutely everything—for the experience.

While this is a personal story rather than a teaching-and-preaching book, both Sar'h and Lauren know a wise master lives within all of us, and if we, as humans, can expand to open to our souls' voices, we can know the ineffable experience of God—a kingdom exists within each of us. Additionally, as a fellow former skeptic and someone who denied her soul's voice for years, for lifetimes, I invite you to read this book with the openness and imagination of a child and to be patient with me, the often-ridiculous human.

I felt it important to share all aspects of myself, not just the attractive ones. It was all part of my journey, after all, and unconditionally loving Self includes ease in acceptance of all parts and pieces, no matter how dark or embarrassing they might appear to others.

As Sar'h says in our first book published, "We must remember the act of being human is wildly courageous in and of itself." She means no matter what we do in our human lives, no matter our thoughts and our actions, or how many times we are perceived to fail, our sheer existence on Earth in physical form is pure magic.

This is where the magic of compassion resides—compassion as honoring everyone and everything—including yourself—without trying to change them, it, or you. It's not about hugs and loving everything crossing our paths. It's letting everyone and everything be where it's at—including yourself—and me—and Earth.

This book is a work of narrative nonfiction—actual stories I experienced. Yet it is only from my perspective. Reality is not an absolute; it changes with every pair of glasses through which it is viewed. Some names have been changed at people's requests. Others insisted on keeping their real names. Other times I choose vagueness—a composite character. That being said, everything in this book did, in fact, occur in my eyes.

---

[7] Maya is a Sanskrit word referring to the illusion of duality, which also creates the illusion of separation between the human experience and soul's divine nature, that of the I am God, too.

Furthermore, I ask the reader not to focus on what's true or real for me, yet where wisdom lies in their own unique soul experience. Self-realization is not a one size fits all experience, and it's the beauty in all of this. Your soul is inimitable, and how you experience the natural unfolding of your self-realization is and will be too.

I hope you enjoy reading these books as much as I enjoyed writing them. Please note while I do not operate fully in linear time I attempted to keep the story in linear format for sake of clarity. In the footnotes, I attempt to define terms used throughout the book. Rather than adopt them, I encourage you to write you own. No matter your feelings on the books or my particular self-realization perspective, it is my dream for everyone to experience the grandest experience life has to offer—the Return to Self—however that looks for them uniquely.

Book One: The Awakening

1 I EXIST

I Exist[8].

It's what I kept coming back to, the only truth that wouldn't crumble under force. I was thirty years old. The walls I so carefully built around myself were caving in.

With one phone call, I knew without a doubt this was the end of life as I knew it. On the horizon, I saw a tidal wave of chaos headed directly toward me. I scrambled in search of the internal truths—the wisdom beyond this singular lifetime—that might serve as my life raft.

I knew only a few things for sure: I was not my thoughts. I was not my body. I was not my emotions swirling and crashing on the shores of this physical reality with wild abandon.

I was not the ever-flowing stories I told myself on a repeating loop. I was not beholden to belief systems, which held clear lines between right and wrong.

I was so many things at once and yet nothing at all.

And, in facing the tidal wave of fast-approaching chaos head on, I sensed a part of me that held steady when the rest fell to pieces—a part of me that could see the reality around me for the illusion it was.

As I stared down the face of the tidal wave in the split second before it broke on my thirty-year-old life, I sensed and knew deeply the quality of Self that was wise beyond my human years, that knew no death.

I heard a whisper, "all you have to do is take a deep breath and sink into me."

It was Sar'h, the voice of my soul. Somehow, totally unexplainable, I knew everything would not only turn out okay, it would also be beyond my wildest human imagination.

---

[8] I Exist, for me, is a state of being, without any attachment to any identities, stories, and expansion beyond a singular reality, such as linear time and dualistic constructs of light and dark, good and evil, right and wrong. It was called the I Am Presence in older texts.

Somehow as a young child I remembered the truth of the I Exist. It was simpler then. Society hadn't yet infiltrated me with the "should" or "supposed to" of life. I was four years old, taking shelter under the kitchen table, wearing nothing but white underwear when I realized it.

My parents were in the living room, rehearsing a familiar scene in which my dad was the perpetrator and my mother the victim. I heard the scene play out from the other room. It felt good to have the protection of the thick oak table over my head. I distinctly remember gazing upon my half-naked body, the body of a child. Funny—I did not feel like a child. In fact, I felt ancient. This was not my body. It must belong to someone else. Nope, I was in it. That I knew. I wore my body like borrowed clothing from another's closet. These emotions of fear, anxiety, and anger at the situation were not mine either. So, what *was* mine, I wondered.

Those emotions belonged to this human body I inhabited. Another lifetime. I have been here before. Many times. More than my four-year-old brain could count. Not in this exact time and space, but with these same souls, playing out these same roles. Only the scenery had changed. This was but one of the realities I existed in. The realization of the I Exist calmed me instantly. I was the fixed point in the many realities swirling around me. I could expand from the I Exist—from the single point in my body of consciousness[9] into the experiences of this human life before contracting back into the single point within the center of my being.

My arguing parents, the unpleasant emotions—they were all simply human details, a tiny drop in the bucket of the vast experiences of the soul. I realized none of my current so-called reality mattered. All that mattered was the I Exist.

I am me. I am nothing else. I am everything else. That simultaneous dichotomy swept over me in instant clarity, followed by mass confusion. There was the first clue, the first kernel of truth, the piece of soul wisdom, which was going to get me through this.

I almost forgot the I Exist—hell, I almost forgot my own soul—yet found my way back to it staring in the face of the wave, the wall of un-relentless water, which loomed before my human self, paralyzed by fear. Life crises tend to have that effect—sending us back into the knowingness of who we truly are and what we are made of.

The childhood memories I had worked so hard to bury flooded back into my awareness, serving as the proverbial breadcrumbs leading me back

---

[9] Body of consciousness refers to my expanded field of awareness beyond the human body and includes the totality of Self. Sometimes El Morya refers to it as the Universe of Self.

to the path of the soul—the one I avoided for all these years.

As a four-year-old child sitting under the kitchen table, I wondered why all the people around me were so intent to live in just one reality when the possibilities were endless. Like me, they dreamed at night, existing in other realms, only to watch it wash away with the daylight. Those dreamlands were no less real than this one. If we existed in so many realities, why were adults so intent to focus only on this singular human life, which to me seemed more of an illusion than the others? Why could they not see what existed beyond?

At the age of seven, I decided to test my theory that realities—or dimensions—could intersect. At the time, turtles fascinated me. My bookshelves were lined with figurines of the mysterious creatures. In true child form, I begged and pleaded with my parents for a pet turtle. I wanted to experience the real thing.

They would not budge, so I decided I would call one into my life. That night I entered a vivid dream in which I spoke to a turtle who introduced himself as Mortimer. I noticed he held the demeanor of a professor.

In the dream, I asked if he would like to come live with me. He said yes and he would like to visit but did not want to live inside the house in a cage. He gently explained to me turtles were meant to live in the wild.

I agreed to his terms, and he told me in the dream he would arrive in three days' time. Three days for a child can feel like three weeks for an adult. Time drug on until it was the day Mortimer was going to show up.

That summer morning, after eating cereal in front of television cartoons, I walked outside with my dog, a dopey blond cocker spaniel named Loopy. Together we rounded the backyard. Loopy used his nose to search.

"There he is!" I yelled at Loopy. He gazed at me in confusion.

A six-inch box turtle slowly made his way through the lush Saint Augustine grass carpeting the backyard, stopping to chew on a blade every now and then. I curiously watched him and wondered if the turtle existed in my imagination or as an actual creature in physical form. I found it terribly difficult to tell the difference at this age; the lines between the realities were too faint to decipher.

I crept up behind him to see if I could touch his patterned shell. When I pressed my finger down, it was hard, and I traced along the ridges of the shell's patterns. The turtle quickly retracted his head and feet when he felt the vibration of my touch.

Full of anticipation, I held myself still, holding my breath and waiting for his head to come back out again. I needed to see his eyes to tell if this turtle was Mortimer. Eventually, his head and feet came back out. His golden eyes seemed to glow as he stared directly at me.

"Mortimer!" I was ecstatic. As I yelled, he retracted into his shell again. I scolded myself for scaring him. I left him in the backyard and ran inside to tell my mom.

"Mom. Mortimer is here. Can I keep him?"

She shrugged her shoulders. If it seemed weird to her, she did not show it. After some thought, my mom guaranteed Mortimer a spot in the small, gated backyard garden. I liked the garden because it contained a large, smooth rock, which served as a perfect perch for a seven-year-old girl.

I lifted him carefully by the shell to place him in the garden, where I would refresh his water bowl and feed him apples and the fat trimmed off dinner steaks. He had a buffet of plants to choose from as well.

Each day, I went into the tiny garden and perched on the rock to converse with Mortimer. Mainly, he talked while I listened, and I only stopped him to ask a few clarifying questions.

One day, Mortimer explained to me turtles—not just land turtles but sea turtles as well—were the keepers of wisdom and long forgotten truths here on Earth. He said turtles stored the wisdom of the ages in the patterns of their protective shells, and the mother and father turtles passed down sacred and often secret codes of wisdom to the baby turtles, so the information remained rooted on Earth, like the trees. Mortimer said ancient cultures knew this and, as a result, highly regarded the animals.

I wondered when and where this knowledge got lost between then and now. It was 1988 in the suburbs of Houston, Texas. We lived in one of the boxes lining our neighborhood street.

As Mortimer told the story, I felt a long way away from home. An overwhelming homesickness caused my stomach to churn. The feeling made no sense to me—I was sitting on a rock in my own backyard.

I reverted back to the safety of my imagination. Delighted to learn of turtles living in the ocean, I imagined them playing in the waves and gliding through the currents of a clear blue sea—something I must experience in real life one day.

Mortimer cleared his throat several times to gain my attention back. Later, adults told me my inability to focus was some sort of human disorder called attention deficit disorder, or ADD. Even later, I realized I was simply in multiple realities and this one got really boring, really quickly.

Once Mortimer pulled me back into the present moment, he became serious, explaining I, too, held codes within me containing long-forgotten knowledge and wisdom.

"Just as turtles are the keepers of wisdom on Earth, you are a keeper of certain truths," he said, attempting to simplify so I could understand. I stared at him, confused.

"Truths kept secret for thousands of years," he added.

Then Mortimer began to speak with me in images and sensations, which were much easier for me to understand. He showed me certain truths, or wisdom, existed inside me, in my soul.

In my third-eye vision, I viewed swirling patterns of numbers and symbols, light made of colors most human eyes could not identify and therefore had no names, and energetic vibrations I could only sense and not see, which expanded in all directions from the center of me, from the I Exist. Whoa. I felt dizzy and steadied myself on the rock.

"Lauren, one day you will share these truths," Mortimer said.

On some level, I believed him. This was the wise Professor Mortimer speaking. I trusted him but was reluctant to claim I held any sort of knowledge. I was only a child.

"Who was going to listen to a child? What did I really know anyway?" I asked myself. My environment frequently seemed extremely dense around me, and often I never bothered to share anything of the sort.

I felt overwhelmed—almost panicked on the human level. In the expanded soul experience, I felt myself sinking into his words and images, swimming through the energetic currents Mortimer tended to radiate like I imaged sea turtles would in the ocean.

Then a question popped into my head. If the mom and dad turtles passed on codes containing wisdom to the baby turtles, where were the parents who passed on the sacred codes holding these truths to me?

It wasn't my human parents, to whom I felt no real connection at the time. And why was this all a secret? Had it not been safe to share? I wondered this but did not ask; I knew Mortimer was not going to tell me.

"Some things we must realize on our own," he told me many times during our visits.

The intense reluctance to exist in this limited physical world I felt before Mortimer showed up ran through my body again. My imaginary world felt more welcoming and natural. I felt freer outside the physical body.

At times, I felt ashamed to be living in human flesh, which seemed icky. I pushed the current thoughts and confusion aside. I really wanted to go swimming with the sea turtles. That night in a dream, I swam with them through a bright blue ocean filled with reefs of neon-green kelp we dined on.

One morning, I walked outside to see Mortimer. He was gone. I imagined him carrying a stick with a red bag tied on the end, like the ones hobos carried in cartoons, as he moved on to the next blond-haired, blue-eyed girl to spread the wisdom of the ages. Keeping good on my word, I didn't go out to search for him.

None of my childhood experiences seemed strange to me. Sensing my soul and dreaming turtles into life, imaginative play, and interacting with energies without physical form felt more natural than the flat mental logic and heavy emotions I witnessed around me.

I engaged in long conversations with trees seemingly holding more knowledge than my parents. I played with energies appearing in every color of the rainbow and beyond, colors I danced with around the backyard.

When a 'color' showed up, I communicated back to the color with images rather than words, speaking to it in its native language. The language of imagery contained so much more information and sensations than limited human words—words with letters I often switched around as I tried to write them on paper.

I don't think my parents noticed any of my highly engaged interactions in our suburban backyard. They most likely wrote it off as childhood play, and because I was an only child, they had nothing to compare it to.

They were too busy playing a strange game. My dad went to a place called 'work' early in the morning and came home late at night, grouchy. He often left with a suitcase during the week, and when he returned on the weekends, he brought me little shampoo bottles from the hotels where he stayed. Later I learned he sold safety supplies to corporations so their workers wouldn't get hurt.

My mom was like a cat: sleeping most of the time. As I got older, I realized she found life disappointing and most of the time feared her own shadow. I watched her try to make peace with being a housewife despite her affinity for writing, reading, and teaching literature. Regardless of her sincere devotion to being my mother, I sensed she never quite got over feeling her gifts and her life were being wasted. I understood, but her forced smiles made my insides hurt nevertheless.

I didn't mind my dad was always gone and my mom slept so much. I disliked it more when they were together, the anger, sadness, and disappointment between them palpable. Their absence afforded me hours alone with the oak tree shading more than half the backyard. I often buried pennies by its roots as tokens of our friendship.

Beings assuming all sorts of shapes and forms would come to visit as well. They all spoke the language of images and sensations. I found comfort in this kind of communication. I especially liked the fairies appearing in flashes of light and the bubbles of pure white consciousness floating through the sunshine rays in the gaps between the branches of the tree.

A play of shadows and light beyond the limits of physical reality sparkled, speaking volumes without the constriction of words.

2 LIFE ON FLAT EARTH

It wasn't until I was eight years old when I learned I needed to hide who I truly was from the people around me—not only the adults around me, but also my peers at the elementary school I attended.

In third grade, the teacher asked us to stand in front of the class and share what made us special or unique. Some kids talked about their dogs, siblings, or favorite television shows. When I stood up to speak, I had nothing planned. It just poured out of me.

"What made me different and unique," I explained, "was I truly cared about the evolution of Earth—both its inhabitants and the nature I loved so much. I actually cared about things beyond my own situation and myself."

It was honest. I had noticed for quite some time people around me, adults and children, seemed completely absorbed in their immediate, physical surroundings and preoccupied with their current human thoughts and emotions.

None of them seemed to see or sense the interconnectedness of everything, and it bothered me immensely. Why could they not see what I saw? Why could they not hear what I heard? Why could they not sense the way I could sense?

As I shared this, I began to cry and felt a massive expansion in my energetic field. It filled the classroom. I was used to having these experiences in my own backyard or talking with Mortimer—but in front of a classroom of eight-year-olds…holy crap!

The teacher and my fellow students were speechless. There was no applause from the audience like there had been for Billy, who before my turn had shared he was special for playing first base. I made my way back to the rug where the other children were sitting cross-legged and hung my head in shame.

"Why couldn't you pretended to be normal?" my human self—or what some people refer to as ego—asked my soul self, who was beginning to identify herself by the name Sar'h.

My soul explained Sar'h was the Hebrew version of the American Sarah, which meant ruler—not over anyone else but a master of or ruler over Self.

I usually only spoke with her in private, but I was raging, and it couldn't wait.

"Please don't do that to me again," I said firmly. "You don't know how hard this being human stuff is!"

I wanted to curl into a ball and disappear. An awkward silence, which felt like it lasted an eternity, loomed over me. The teacher called on another student next. She stood up confidently and said, "I am special because I am adopted."

The entire class erupted in laughter because everyone knew she had two older brothers, and they all looked alike. I witnessed the energy of the room around me shift, and I felt better.

Then it occurred to me I might be the only child in the classroom—probably in the whole school—who physically saw laughter dissolve discomfort, the only child aware of the energetic dynamics of the classroom.

As I witnessed the energy of the classroom shift, feeling entirely alien and alone, I vowed then and there to never share from the soul space again. I never wanted to feel that kind of shame again. It was better to pretend to fit in, although I knew how bad I was at it.

This was how I was going to survive in this cruel world. I learned in this moment, as a human you were expected to conform to a set of predetermined social norms. You were allowed some wiggle room to be different, but it couldn't be too far out there.

As a human being, you were expected to adhere to a pattern of goal setting and accomplishment. I did not understand the rigidity of this behavior. Creation was not a linear process; it did not come from thinking and hard work. I proved it with my turtle experiment.

It made me furious I was expected to operate in such antiquated ways, and I could not show who I truly was from the expanded soul experience. The world around me was maddening. I hated everything, especially the slap in the face that was living in a flat Earth mentality.

The damage of the experience firmly taught me never to speak of things that did not exist in the physical world again. I cried myself to sleep for several nights after the event.

Shortly thereafter, I asked my parents for a pet gerbil. After I launched a full-lobby strategy with handwritten notes and a presentation; they agreed. I was learning how the human world worked and found I could be quite talented at the manipulation, which passed for competency in this world.

My mom and I picked out a soft, brown female at the pet store.

I loved the way her whiskers and nose twitched when she stood on her hind legs to look at me from behind the glass. Together, my mom and I picked out a cage, toys, and food and brought her home.

I found my mom really loving that day and noticed I was enjoying her company too. We were laughing and joking. She felt like a best friend who never judged me, and it made me smile. Maybe she was not my "real" mother, but she could be an excellent friend.

Later, I realized there is no such thing as a mother and it was simply a role to play on Earth's stage. It took the sting out of never being hugged or played with as a child.

"What would you like to name her?" my mom asked when we got home.

"I'm going to name her Sar'h," I said.

"Oh, after your new friend, Sarah?" my mom asked, referring to a new girl in school I was desperate to make friends with.

"Yes," I lied, knowing she would not understand.

That night I placed Sar'h, the voice of my soul, into the gerbil and the gerbil into a glass cage.

"I'm going to try to be a normal child," I told the gerbil. "I'm on the verge of making new friends, and I cannot risk another embarrassment. It's social suicide."

Sar'h understood and wished me well. I didn't consciously hear my soul voice again until I was eleven years old, when we put the gray-haired, long-toothed Sarah the gerbil to sleep.

The vet explained to me, as tears rolled down my chin, that Sarah's three-year life-span was much longer than most gerbils'. I didn't tell him I was not only crying for my gerbil, but also because I knew it was time to bring Sar'h, my soul voice, back into my life.

It worried me to have to live in two worlds once again. By this time, I established a tight-knit circle of girlfriends — ones I did not want to lose by being too weird — yet something inside me told me I was ready.

These childhood memories began to light the way back to the path of the soul—my wiser, pre-programming child self was educating my thirty-year-old self to ditch the programming plaguing my life since then.

There was the memory of the I Exist—the fixed point within my soul within the body of consciousness, the totality of Self. With the memory came the understanding all human pain and suffering was only a drop in the bucket of the vast experience of the soul. Although it might hurt like hell in the moment, soon the illusion of human suffering would dissolve within the ever-changing tides of my consciousness, or awareness of Self.

There was the inner knowing there were parts of myself I needed to get to know again. The human self was one voice in a complex web that made up Self, the all I am. The other major voice, for me, was that of the soul—the wise master residing within all of us, if we chose to claim it.

I understood, at age thirty, I needed to invite my soul voice back into the conversation of my life to move forward. The memories brought back the awareness that imagination and dreams were two senses, tools I could use to mold and shape my reality. I remembered intuition was also a language of the soul, a form of soul communication to which I was already open to.

I held an inner knowing many more sophisticated senses—experiences of feeling beyond the five human senses and beyond human thoughts and emotions—existed inside me if I could find my way back to the soul. The memories reminded me I possessed an innate ability to work with and interpret energies—that my relationship with energy was far beyond my intellectual capabilities.

As I remembered these abilities, I realized I used these gifts daily—I hadn't lost the abilities, only the awareness of them. In the memories, I also learned I spoke the language of images and sensations fluently as a child.

Like any language you don't use enough, the translations move into the back of the file folders of awareness. The knowledge does not leave, yet cobwebs must be dusted off, and atrophied muscles must be flexed repeatedly for the wisdom to return to human, physical awareness.

I also realized every human had access to his or her soul, the guru or master voice within, just as I did. It only required consciousness or awareness of Self to realize the expanded nature of the soul.

I knew without doubt everyone had access to these same senses and abilities if they opened themselves up, if they allowed them to flow inward, unfiltered by human thoughts and emotions.

That was why it was so maddening to me as a child to learn people could not see the potentials and possibilities, lying dormant within them. The unrealized potential always laying just outside their body of consciousness, outside their fields of awareness.

I continued my search for wisdom to support me through the impending flood—scanning my memories for any hints—even the slightest, tiniest clue.

3 SAR'H RETURNS

With the onset of puberty, my awareness and experiences with energy intensified. When I became a woman, the prophetic dreams and visions strengthened, much to my discomfort. I found myself more sensitive than ever to external energies, in addition to the mood swings common among teenagers.

I was empathetic to the extreme. If a classmate was sad, I felt it in every cell of my body. I absorbed his or her pain and suffering as if it were my own, and then I reflected it back to the person involuntarily, which made me no fun to be around. I found no reprieve at home. Sad mother. Angry father.

I could not distinguish where my energy field ended and another's began. I could not discern where my teenage human emotions ended and the consciousness of my soul began. It was confusing and exasperating.

As a result, I ate. I ate when I was sad, stressed, angry—anything. I ate when those around me felt discomfort in any form. My house happened to be filled with copious amounts of junk food and soda, available at all times.

In seventh grade, the school nurse weighed me in front of the whole class; it was some Arnold Schwarzenegger fitness program that made it into the public schools.

"One hundred and twenty-seven pounds," the nurse called out to the entire classroom as I turned a deep shade of red.

I had not realized how overweight I had become. I weighed a good thirty pounds more than most of my classmates. I searched inside for an answer as to how this had occurred without me realizing it. The truth I discovered was my soul was not inside my body. Instead, she hovered like a nebulous cloud above it. It felt too painful to stay in the physical body while it absorbed the feelings of the moody teenagers and unconscious parents surrounding me.

The weight served as a completely ineffective barrier to the emotions of others. I retreated into my imagination, into the nonphysical realms, which is what I did when things became intense. I tried various things to connect my soul back with my body but couldn't quite figure out a lasting solution. My body continued to feel like a shell—a separate being walking around empty and on autopilot.

Throughout junior high and during my freshman year in high school, I created a small group of trusted friends. Music was our common denominator. I grew up listening to Carol King, Bob Dylan, Johnny Cash, Paul Simon, Motown Records' artists, and the Beatles.

I loved listening to and interacting with music as it transported me to the place of no time and no space. It was also a place where I felt understood by my friends on the spinning vinyl records. The first time I heard the Beatles song "Tomorrow Never Knows," I was blown away.

When John Lennon sings the opening lyrics, "Turn off your mind, relax and float downstream. It is not dying, it is not dying," I could feel consciousness in the words.

Later in the song Lennon sings, "Listen to the color of your dreams." It wasn't just drug talk, as those around me said; it was what I had been doing my whole childhood, sober.

In seventh or eighth grade, I heard Jimi Hendrix for the first time. The way he played guitar, the energy flowing from the amplifier, was all soul voice, and it stirred something inside me I could not quite describe at the time. It was the sensation of stuck energy inside me being freed. This music was the first time I experienced art in a way that moved me at both the human and the soul level of experience. My new friends could relate, and it was amazing.

For the first time, I had something to talk with my friends about that created a connection. For years I longed to have a connection with my peers but never found the right frequency to ride into the conversation on without it seeming awkward or forced. I didn't feel like an outsider for once, or at least less of one.

Music made me belong.

After school, my music-loving friends and I convened in one of our bedrooms, locked the parents out, and listened to the greats like Jimi and Led Zeppelin and the new stuff like Nirvana and White Zombie.

I dyed my hair black and wore combat boots with dresses or jeans and flannel, imitating the style of Courtney Love. I spent my spare time in garages with teenage boys with long hair, learning to play instruments.

We hid in the neighborhood park bushes, smoking cigarettes and swag weed and eating psychedelic mushrooms we had picked from cow patties.

In an altered state, I read a book aloud called *Das Energi* by Paul

---

[10] Williams, Paul. *Das Energi*. New York: Elektra Books, 1973.

Williams[10]. It was a collection of poetry fusing rock and roll with Eastern philosophy and New Age consciousness. It was the only book Jac Holzman published through Elektra Records, which had introduced Jim Morrison and the Doors to the world.

My new group of friends and I enjoyed the magic of immersing ourselves into the world of rock music. It was a lovely escape from the sterile, florescent-lit box that was our school.

When I wasn't with my friends, I studied. Not schoolwork—I completed it before I left the school building. I studied any book with esoteric knowledge I could get my hands on. This was pre-internet and Amazon, so I was limited to what I could find in the library. We lived in suburbia, so there wasn't much selection beyond major world religions. Growing up, my mom read me Bible stories, and I attended weekly Catholic education classes.

I felt a strong connection with this Jesus man my mom always talked about, yet I knew something was missing. The people around me used their minds to interpret the stories of his life, when these stories were intended to arouse something in the soul.

Additionally, half of the Bible seemed to be missing because it only showed a male perspective and nothing was ever mentioned about reincarnation. It's a hell of a lot easier to control people who think they only have one life ending in heaven or hell.

When I quickly hit my limits at the library and church, I convinced my mother to take me to the large Book Stop store in the city. I remember I lit up like a Christmas tree when I walked the aisles of the New Age section for the first time.

Despite her strict Catholic upbringing, my mom understood me enough to let me pick out any book I wanted. I was not ever going to be steered into some concept or belief system that did not feel right, and I think she always knew it.

My mom believed in Jesus and his teaching through the church in a loose, yet devoted sort of way, but she encouraged me to learn about other schools of thought. It was a true childhood luxury. I rabidly digested anything I could get my hands on. Astrology, tarot cards, runes, Wicca, witchcraft, psychics, metaphysics, ghosts, mediums—I read it all, but it wasn't what I was looking for.

Eastern philosophy and yoga, which has currently taken the Occident by storm, hadn't made it to the suburbs of Houston, Texas, in the early 1990s. The only knowledge from the Orient available to me was basic books on Buddhism and Hinduism—both felt entirely too masculine and too mental. I knew it wasn't what I was looking for. I gravitated toward books that allowed for moving beyond the mind rather than going into its inner workings.

Many of the books were interesting, but one lit up in my thirteen-year-old hands—*The 21 Lessons of Merlyn: A Study in Druid Magic & Lore* by Douglas Monroe—the copy I still have on my bookshelf today. [11]

It was a dense, scholarly book with more than four hundred pages. The cover depicted a young blond boy sitting on a rock while a wise, silver-haired teacher wearing a long robe taught him something under a grand oak tree. The picture stirred something inside me. It looked an awful lot like me perched on the rock talking to Mortimer in the garden some years ago.

"That's really strange," I thought, feeling the stirring of wisdom in my soul— an ever so strange, yet so familiarly distinct sensation I call *remembering*.

When I started reading the text, it wasn't the words but the images transported me to a time and place where I lived completely connected with nature—where magic, dreams, imagination, and the bending of time and space existed as common knowledge.

With my eyes closed, I smelled the fresh dampness in the air. It was cool, spring-like. Everything around me was bright green and alive. The snow had recently melted, and it seemed as if the forest was vibrating with celebration.

In this time and space, I was a young woman, an adult. I wore a long, flowing white dress and walked barefoot on a carpet made of damp, bright green moss. My long, dark hair was the color of my father's, and it turned a shade of red in the sunlight like my mother's.

In this place, my gifts for working with energy—my ability to create things seemingly out of thin air and to feel others at such a deep level—was not only normal but also highly regarded. It felt so real. I was there, and yet I felt thousands of years and thousands of miles away, simultaneously.

I went so deeply into this transformative experience simply holding the book in my hand and hours passed as I lay on my bedroom floor with my dog, a black cocker spaniel named Kacee, who never veered too far from my side.

Some of the words in the book spoke directly to me. In the introduction, the author suggested if you could read the book with the open-mindedness of a child, you would receive more from it. Monroe understood children were open to the nonphysical world, as I had been. He also said Druids were called tree people—*Druid* literally meant "men of the oak."

An image of my relationship with the great oak in my own backyard popped into my inner vision. Furthermore, the book mentioned the soul, a word surprisingly missing from other texts, and the soul's ability to take

---

[11] Monroe, Douglas. *The 21 Lessons of Merlyn: A Study in Druid Magic & Lore*. Saint Paul: Llewellyn Publications, 1992.

various human forms through the reincarnation process. Finally!

I jumped the massive leap in awareness without thought—my soul had lived many lives, many incarnations, and I was here once again. Sar'h was not just me, but also the dark-haired woman in the woods, and so, so many others.

I was so many people at once. I was everything, and I was nothing. There was the sensation again. Whoa. Spinning. If I tried to wrap my brain around it, it felt too confusing; on a sensory level, it made perfect sense.

Besides the Druid philosophy, spells, and rituals, most of which were too mental for me to digest, the book featured the story of an orphan boy named Arthur, who meets a teacher he calls Merlyn who shows him, like any great teacher, where to look, not what to see.

In the book, Arthur undergoes a series of experiences or initiations facilitated by his merlin—merlin is actually a title, not a person—before realizing at the end he is, in fact, destined to be king. Merlyn never shares this knowledge directly with Arthur; instead, Arthur must figure it out for himself.

"Some things we must realize on our own," Mortimer had said. The words reverberated through my body of consciousness once again. As they did, my whole nervous system re-wired itself yet again.

Instead of the literal story, I focused on the energy between the words, reading the book with the consciousness of my soul rather than within the confines of my human mind.

I saw how Arthur's story serves as a parable for self-realization, what some call enlightenment. I understood Arthur's noble status wasn't about ruling over a kingdom of people but rather being the ruler of your own kingdom—Self.

The knowingness repeated in a whisper—Sar'h—Hebrew for ruler or princess, the feminine version — a ruler over the kingdom of Self. The knowledge came into my physical body like a steam train.

At thirteen years old, I knew this was what I was here on Earth to experience—I did not know yet it was called self-realization. I simply did not have the words for it yet; they had never been handed to me. Realization, or enlightenment, was only a sensation of knowing and remembering who I was, and what I was here to be.

At the time, the concept was only a sensation that felt real and true, more so than the world I happened to be living in. The information, or wisdom, rather, began to click beyond the density of my human mind, emotions, and physical body.

I wondered, "How do you get up and go to the sterile public school after an experience such as this?" And then I took a deep and consciousness breath knowing you just do and cry on the inside the whole time you're there, knowing it is all a ridiculous façade.

You cry inside *and* you know why the caged bird still sings. You will be able to ring the bell of Freedom one day. It just won't be today, you tell yourself.

The book also confirmed some childhood experiences for me. In the book, Monroe said the Druids knew the nonphysical or other world was every bit as real and tangible as the physical world, and one affected the other constantly. It was the first time I saw in written word something I knew so clearly from the source of who I Am.

It brought to the surface a deep soul desire to write down these things no one wanted to talk about. I did not need to teach or convince anyone of anything but to lend words to an experience that many go through suffering in silence and confusion.

I wanted to remind others they were not mad. They had not lost their minds. They did not need to turn around and go back when the soul journey got too scary, too intense. I held a passion for reminding others in similar experiences to simply let go and experience themselves beyond the perception of separation—beyond the dualistic construct of internal human and external divine.

Additionally, in the book, Merlyn speaks to Arthur about a universal picture language—communicating in visual imagery beyond human physical sight—a language of which I remembered I was fluent in—energetic communication—how my soul communicated information, or wisdom, to the human part of me.

My soul also communicated in sensations that lay beyond biological senses, such as taste, smell, sight, touch, and hearing. Instead of hearing, I listened deeply. I could reach within myself and touch something with no physical form. I could see—through this communication— a life of freedom was available to me if I allowed it to be so.

My soul rarely spoke to me in words, choosing images and sensations instead, which I then translated into words as necessary. The information seemed to come in through wisdom packets I had to unravel with *gnost*, or inner knowing, rather than with my human mind.

"There is soul wisdom, and there is common knowledge. Discernment defines the experience, at will," Sar'h would interject in a radical sensation I translated into a quote with energy placed between the words.

Whatever she shared was always simple. Soul wisdom is always uncomplicated and vast and without the charge of positivity or negativity; it's impact flows in its subtle neutrality.

The book also distinguished between the perceived reality of the collective human consciousness and the expanded perception of the soul—confirming my experience in the classroom at age eight. Even though I knew I did not make these things up, it was a comfort to read about how other people saw and experienced the same things as me, but in their unique way. Reading this book, I also realized there were others like me out there somewhere. I knew I would meet them someday when I left the suburbs of Houston to travel the world. It excited me to no end.

However, the book had its limitations. It implied only celibate men could experience authority over Self, or enlightenment. It talked about enlightened beings Jesus, whom I now call Yeshua, and Buddha, yet I knew there were women who had accomplished mastery over Self as well. I knew celibacy and a dick were not requirements. Come on.

Although I could see why most would forgo children during the time when the self-realization lifetime descended into the physical plane in a radically passionate expression of the soul's desire to know itself as God. You simply cannot have enough time with your Self in this magical space, and you don't necessarily want to share with others having another experience fully in the illusion of maya.

I reclaimed my feminine authority another way. It showed up in a book called *The Witch in Every Woman: Reawakening the Magical Nature of the Feminine to Heal, Protect, Create, and Empower* by Laurie Cabot, which I discovered at the age of sixteen. The dedication of the book simply stated, "To Sovereignty."

The word *sovereignty* rolled around my tongue like a marble. It is to this day one of my favorite words. I realized it was another way to talk about the self-governing nature of the soul or the authority over Self as I read in King Arthur's story, as is recognized in the personification of my soul— Sar'h.

Cabot also talks about femininity and sex in a way that resonated in harmony with my soul voice. Cabot writes,

"A woman's entire existence is sexual, her every move a sexual expression. If she decides to enjoy sex with a partner, she should understand it is an enhancement to an innate sensibility she already possesses and enjoys. When it comes to sex, a modern woman must say to herself... 'I am sovereign.' ...Sexual loving is an integral part of her nature."[12]

I wanted to write Monroe a letter and ask him why women were left from his story. I also found the spells in many of the books I read, especially ones affecting the lives of others or worse manipulated them— not respecting sovereignty of another—did not resonate with me at all. I checked in with Sar'h, the ultimate authority over my Self. I found these answers through the song of my soul: to be sovereign you must also recognize the sovereign nature of everyone around you. Sex should be an

---

[12] Cabot, Laurie, and Jean Mills. *The Witch in Every Woman: Reawakening the Magical Nature of the Feminine to Heal, Protect, Create, and Empower.* New York: Dell Publishing, 1997.

act of self-love. Period. The end.

It always seemed so much easier to go to the source within for answers to my big questions. However, the stories contained in these two books— not the spells and exercises, but the parables—helped me confirm and reclaim pieces of myself at an impressionable age, pieces I might have lost in the confines of the modern, mind-based world I lived in, and I am grateful to have found them.

My esoteric studies relieved the awkwardness of my early teenage years. Magic and nature were the saving graces in a flat, noisy, mind-based world. I never shared too much with my friends. If they happened to see one of my books, I showed them some spell to distract them or buried them in stories so complex they would lose me. I certainly wasn't going to bring up self-realization; I'm not even sure I could have spoken about it in a way that made sense. Music was the perfect way to connect, as talking during it was highly discouraged.

As I relaxed more into my true nature, I eased back into my physical body, and I found it uncomfortable to be overweight. My parents were also overweight, especially my dad. He had a round Santa Claus belly to match his silver hair, which he said turned from black to white when he jumped from a plane in Vietnam. When I told my dad I wanted to lose weight, he insisted it was in our DNA or part of our ancestral heritage.

"We're big-boned," he told me, but I knew better.

I held an understanding no one was ever bound to his or her DNA or ancestral lineage, and it could be changed with consciousness, or pure soul awareness without complicated steps or procedures. You just let all those old ancestral ties go and move on.

My mom saw how serious I was, and after talking with a friend, she found the name of a personal trainer in the area. He owned a gym in Katy, Texas. I had never taken to group sports or any after-school activities really, so I went to see this trainer while my peers ran track, played soccer, or rehearsed plays after school.

Over the next two years, the personal trainer changed my concepts of health and self-esteem entirely. He not only showed me how to work out but also how to eat. I found it so much easier to connect my soul within my body when my body became a safe and pleasant space to inhabit. The physical exercise moved the stuck energy causing the extra weight, and changing my eating habits creating a less toxic environment within the body for the soul to reside.

Yet as quickly as I discovered this gem of a realization, it was thrown to the side as well as my soul's voice—once again. I was headed straight into my drug addiction experience, and my soul wouldn't reconnect with my physical body for another decade.

BECOMING SAR'H

4 THE ADDICTION YEARS

It took some years but by seventeen years old my ugly duckling turned into a swan. I had muscle and a size-two figure. I let my hair grow back to its natural blond. The guys who had made fun of me and called me Shamu, the whale, now drooled over me, and I was happy to play my new role.

With all the attention and new friends, I left my esoteric studies and my music friends. I was popular now and didn't have time for such things as enlightenment, merlins, rock and roll, and certainly not my soul. My parents bought me a cherry-red convertible. Instead of Jimi and Zeppelin, I blasted Tupac and Timbaland from the tape deck.

The summer before my senior year, I met a guy about two years older than me who attended a college nearby. We spent every summer day together, smoking weed, drinking beer, swimming, and playing cards with our friends, who also had nothing to do.

He introduced me to sex, but it was his cocaine I fell for. The first time I did a line of coke with him, I knew I was hooked. It made me feel like I was all human, all the time. I was confident. I was not empathic to the people around me. I did not see or sense energetic designs anymore. I couldn't have cared less about anything but my immediate surroundings and myself.

"This must be how humans feel every day," I thought. The notion was absurd, yet it fit into my experiences perfectly.

Later a healer would transport me back to the moment my drug addiction went from dabbling into full blown insanity. I can remember it so clearly now from the expanse of the soul perspective. It was my junior year. I was at a party with my friends. We were standing around an old warehouse owned by one of the cool kid's parents. We all showed up in our parent-purchased vehicles and everyone brought whatever mind-altering substance they could find to share.

I remember feeling so out of place, so separated from physical reality—a general sense of not knowing why I was there in this popularity contest party.

With a cold Bud Light beer in one hand, I held a joint in another. When I took a drag off of it, I sensed a strong force that came down over my energetic field. I felt like I was hit with a baseball bat. I remember the lights going off and my body going down to the ground with a heavy thud.

To those in witness, it appeared I only blacked out from the drugs and alcohol for a split second before getting back up, but what occurred in the blackout was so much more.

There was a group of souls, about twelve of them. Each of the souls had experienced human lifetimes in which they either accidently or purposely killed themselves through overdosing. Unbeknownst to my human self at the time, I agreed to walk them through the experience of drug addiction and show them first-hand how to escape the perceived prison of addiction.

It was in this moment, my soul went out of body completely and agreed to provide this service to these souls who had become so lost in the astral realms after death they could not find their own way back to the natural evolution of lifetimes, having been through a full life review. Instead, these souls found themselves stuck in the near-earth realms reincarnating from a space where you do not have the time and angelic support needed to make a solid decision and conscious choice of your next incarnation. It is something I will never do again, yet to put in human terms, it was a favor I repaid. Now I know I do not have to repay anyone for anything from any lifetime.

I wouldn't remember until I was thirty-two that I once took my own life and dove deeply into the self-created slums of the near-earth realms— ones I made my way through, after a time of being extremely lost in the density of despair lining these halls. The movie *What Dreams May Come* was not fiction for me. I lived it. And to find my own way out, various souls had taken the time to show me through example, a way to exit this space, return to my angelic family, and heal.

By eighteen years old, the Lauren human persona hit full-blown addict status, and it timed perfectly with my freshman year in college. When sniffing coke wasn't enough, I spiraled out of control into the designer drug buffet readily available across the university campus. If I was going to allow myself to experience the darkness of addiction, I was going to go all in. Three years, a felony drug charge, and a rehab stint later, I decided to get clean.

And in the process of finding my freedom, in breaking the chains of addiction, I wrote. I wrote daily a journal to myself. I wrote a dialogue between my soul self and my human self. And as I wrote, I showed the twelve souls I had taken under my wings what it meant to Return to Self, to walk out of the prison cell that really had no lock on it after all.

I played a role—one I realized was conscious years later. I wasn't actually repaying a debt, I saw in my newfound awareness. I was making good on a promise to myself. Because I had found my way out of this dark and twisted astral realm, I said, "If I can ever help other souls find their own way out, I will take the opportunity to do so."

In my current view, I realized I never lost myself in the addiction. I realized indeed, this was an act of consciousness, and a precise creation of the soul. But at the time, the experience was vicious, and it felt like a living hell to quit using. Most days I walked two steps forward, only to be blown down to the bottom of the staircase once again.

Yet by age twenty, I found I traded one addiction for another—a socially acceptable disease called success. Previously limited to the Western world, the success addiction seems to have spread to virtually every corner of the Earth with the onset of a technocratic world and to anyone with a smart phone.

In my early twenties, I dove into the deep end of the American dream. I finished my undergraduate degree in journalism and graduated with honors at age twenty-one. I went on to work for a United States senator, and for award-winning newspapers in South Carolina, Georgia, and back home in the Houston area. I was on the hamster wheel of external fulfillment, and I could not get enough of my next fix.

By the age of twenty-four, I'd made my way back to Texas, again working in politics. At twenty-five, I met my future husband. After earning my master's degree and graduating in one of the top ten slots, I married my husband, and I started my new career as a nonprofit lobbyist, where I was quickly being promoted up the chain of command. I was so convinced of my belief in success as a path I even fooled myself.

Just like any experience in maya, you have to get so lost in the game that is duality, so lost in believing your role on the Earth's stage is your singular reality in order to have the experience of returning to Self once again—knowing it was all an illusion or a play you forgot you were acting in and actually believed the role was really you!

Just like that—in the blink of an eye—a decade flashed across the movie screen of my limited human existence in but a few short paragraphs. Then at thirty years old, I looked at myself in the mirror and realized I was living the singular human life I had found so offensive as a child and teen.

There was no magic, imagination, or play in my life. My soul voice was nowhere to be found, and my human brain and body were preprogrammed, goal-setting, and accomplishing machines. I was a living, breathing machine—one with only a tiny spark of consciousness buried so deep I could not find it among the rubble of 'success'.

So where had I lost it, this sense of Self? Where and when had I exited the road to self-realization? When I felt into it, I realized it—the soul or master voice had never really left. It was shelved, stepping in only in times of major crises and then returning to the shelf, waiting for me, Lauren, the human, to recognize her.

The soul is so patient with the human expression of itself. The soul has such unwavering passion and unconditional love for the human—so much so if the human says, "Hey, I'm going to have the experiences of doing drugs, partying with the cool kids, becoming a wild lobbying success, whatever," the soul says, "Okay, I'll be here when you get back."

In some cases, this can take lifetimes. For others, all it takes is a crack in the human self for the soul to return. It can be an actual physical trauma or an emotional one. What the human views as a tragedy is so often an opportunity for the soul to seep back in through the cracks. "Bump and fill" is what I heard it called later. My tragedy or opportunity—however I chose to perceive it—was quickly approaching.

At thirty years old, my life changed in an instant—with a phone call informing me my dad had slipped into a coma and would probably never wake up. Those childhood memories resurfaced, and my soul jumped at the opportunity to come back into my human's field of awareness.

I realized I could no longer hide behind the facade of success. The dam I had built to shut out the chaos of consciousness—the awareness of who I truly was—crumbled, and there was nothing I could do to stop it. I was unaware of the details while completely aware my life was about to change entirely.

Between the summers of 2011 and 2013, I lost everything that mattered to me and, as a result, my human identity. I felt like I died, yet it was only the actor in the play of human life who had died, and I wasn't quite sure who was left standing.

My father. My career. My husband. And more importantly, I was about to flush an entire set of belief systems down the toilet. I would be left with nothing but the I Exist and the few proverbial fairytale breadcrumbs back to the path of the soul I collected from childhood and adolescence. And I was going to need a stiff drink.

5 THE CALLS

I spent the extreme heat of August and September 2011 in a frigid room at an intensive care unit in a small Texas town. In hindsight, it must have been bizarre to see me driving from the city to the neighboring community twice daily in the triple-digit, heat advisory weather bundled in a sweat suit.

I was too tired to care. It took all my energy to swipe my greasy blond hair into a bun. Makeup was out of the question, despite the dark circles that pooled like sinkholes under my eyes.

I felt like the walking dead, like the heroin addicts I saw on Hastings Street during a vacation to Vancouver. Yes, they were technically alive, but you could see their souls disassociated completely from their bodies. I saw the same soulless face looking back at me in the mirror each morning before I made the drive to sit next to my father's half-alive, half-dead body.

The nurses and doctor—if I could ever find him—probably thought I was in my early twenties, maybe a student, which in their defense was exactly what I looked like. I never took the time to tell them otherwise. It didn't matter. My belief system unraveled before my eyes. I was watching myself from outside myself.

It didn't matter I skipped a grade; that I overcame a severe drug addiction; that I moved to Washington, DC, with nothing but a suitcase and dream; that I worked for eleven dollars an hour at my first job, living in a four-hundred-square-foot housing project; that now, at the age of thirty, I successfully led a team on a government relations initiative for cancer research and prevention funding.

None of it mattered now that my dad was dying. If it had been a week ago, I might be compelled to tell them how important I was. Even in the face of death, I found I could laugh at my own absurdities. I had been collecting my successes like I collected the buffet of drugs I dined on in college. An addiction prison is an addiction prison, no matter the substance.

The thing is, I knew my dad was going to die. I woke up one morning a few months before he ended up in the hospital. I think it was around April that year. I remember shooting straight up into a seated position in bed when a voice said loud and clear, "Your dad is going to die."

I began to cry, and then I remembered a strange voice with no physical body telling me something so important was crazy, forgetting all about Sar'h and our previous conversations. I stuffed the information back down where it belonged—buried with the other facts I did not want to face.

I'd heard the voice before—it didn't come from within; it was external and usually came from my left side. I was so far into the singular human experience, so far away from the expanse of my true nature felt in childhood, it never occurred to me it was my soul speaking to me again.

The last time the voice spoke with that much conviction was in the height of my drug addiction. It was 1999, twelve years prior. I was eighteen and living in an apartment near campus. My house was a carousel of drugs, dealers, and addicts. In a rare moment, I found myself alone and coming down off the latest three-day coke binge.

The voice said, "You need to get everything out of your house." It meant the drugs, paraphernalia, and the cast of shady characters. I heard it loud and clear, yet I chalked it up to being severely tired and strung out. Instead of cleaning out the apartment, I took a sleeping pill and went to bed. As I was starting to drift off to sleep, police, some dressed in all black and with large guns, broke down my door and ransacked my house. They could have simply knocked, and I would let them in, too tired and too strung out to care.

I remembered the voice played a part in my whole life, even though as an adult I often ignored it or was too fucked up to listen to it. It wasn't until I was in the hospital with my half-dead father I realized it was the voice of my soul—the one I had discarded to party with the cool kids and later in the name of success. In these instances, the voice existed outside my body, but it was about to reenter through the cracks of my human self, created by the immense grief I was experiencing as I watched my father die a slow, painful death.

The day before I got the call that changed everything, the "why-I-mattered" list was what kept me going. I told myself I was the definition of American success and living the dream. Like some cheesy self-help guru, I listed off my success superpowers when I became anxious over things like discovering a typo in a company-wide e-mail or gaining three pounds on vacation.

I could work my smart phone in my sleep, convince legislators to vote my way, work sixty-hour weeks, and still have the time to run and diet myself into a size-four designer dress. I reminded myself of all the things that created the undeniable proof I was a wild success. After the call, I couldn't fathom I'd ever actually cared about these things. I was dumbfounded at how much can change in any given moment.

The day of the call was like any other day for me. I walked out of work, got into my car, and called my dad on the way home like I did every weekday. Yes, my dad told me he was having a minor procedure that day, but he insisted I not take off work for something so minor.

My dad had recently learned the scar tissue in his throat had built up so much, he was breathing out of a hole the size of a pen tip. A legally designated disabled veteran by the federal government, the doctors speculated it was from exposure the Agent Orange in the Vietnam War, something he had volunteered for, but no one really knew for sure. My dad was also overweight and tended to ignore his diabetes—another thing he picked up in Vietnam.

The procedure was described to me as simply placing a stint into his throat to open it back up. It only took a short time to complete. We were not aware of the risks. When my dad picked up the hospital phone, he sounded okay.

"Better not to visit," he said. "Doctor says I shouldn't talk much. I'll be out tomorrow."

"Okay, Dad. I'll come tomorrow and pick up dinner."

The next morning, I received the call from his girlfriend to come quickly to the hospital. She couldn't tell me anything except to hurry, so I did. The shock in her voice told me something was terribly wrong.

"The surgery didn't work," the doctor said flatly when I arrived, desperate. "His throat has closed up and cut off oxygen to the brain. We have induced a coma. He may not wake up, Lauren."

It felt as if someone had put a pitchfork down my throat and into my stomach, where they began to twist it. I doubled over in pain. I may never get to say good-bye. I couldn't control my agony. Then I couldn't control my fear. Then I couldn't control my anger. My feelings oscillated wildly. I need to blame someone — myself, the doctor, anyone!

"When will he wake up?" I asked again. "I have to tell him I love him!"

But the doctor said he did not know if he would ever wake up.

"Give me a percentage," I said. It's something my boss always asked about the chance of passage of the legislation I was working on at any given moment.

"Fifty," he said. I could tell he felt it was much less by the look in his eyes.

Right then and there, time stopped. I felt my heart turn to glass and shatter into a thousand tiny shards. I watched them helplessly bounce and scatter across the cold hospital floor.

My dad's girlfriend was beside me, but I felt completely and utterly alone in the world. Even though I had a husband and a mother, I'd never felt a connection to them the way I did with my dad, and where were they now?

My parents divorced when I was twenty-one years old, and they never spoke. My husband only knew parts of me, the ones he wanted to see, the ones I was willing to share. Besides, he always seemed to be at work during this whole ordeal—also in the addiction to success that keeps us from really living our lives, stuck in a loop of earn and spend.

Neither of them ever quite got me the way my dad did. No one did. At the time, he was my one connection to this world that did not feel forced or surface level. And I knew I was about to lose him—in this form, anyway— forever.

It's true my dad and I hadn't been close when I was growing up. But when I was sixteen years old, my dad went into the hospital for triple bypass surgery. The doctors said he would be in for a week. Eight months and many near-death experiences later, he finally came home. Something had changed in him, opening me up to getting to know him. He had connected with his soul too.

It held the opposite effect for my mom. After he got back onto his feet and retired from the job that took him away at all hours, my mother left him when I was finally sober, twenty-one, and a senior in college. It was for her own soul reasons, and I understood completely. That was the silver lining in the divorce. It's when my dad's and my true friendship began.

Something was different in him when he got better. No longer hard as nails and overbearing, my dad became a gentle giant. I was able to share myself completely with him in a way I'd never shared with anyone before. He was present with me in a way he never had been when I was growing up. I found, much to my surprise, I really liked him both as a person—he was quite funny and a rule breaker—and at the soul level.

I found when I looked at his gray-blue eyes, identical to mine, I felt a connection to where I'd come from—not as a human but as a soul. He reflected back to me something I did not yet see inside myself—a strength and ability to create big—to take creations from the ethers and bring them into this physical world.

He also reflected back to me a way of being—an existence. My dad was not only a large man physically, but you also could feel his presence radiate from miles away. He taught me to never dim my shine and to never shrink myself to fit into situations. Instead, he suggested allowing situations to adapt to my expansiveness.

Later I would learn I chose my parents for specific reasons before I came back to Earth in this life. I chose my father for his connection to my angelic or soul family and my mother for a connection to the bloodline I had been born into for so many lifetimes. As a child, I didn't understand what brought them together; it seemed to make no logical sense. The more I remembered who I was, the more the dots connected.

If I had the choice to be friends with anyone in the world, I would choose the soul inhabiting my dad's physicality. I often chose him over nights out with friends. I knew having Robin Hutton as my father was something special on this strange planet. I would live in an ice fishing hole if he had asked me to, and the intensive care unit didn't feel too far off.

My dad's lifeless body was covered in ice packs in an effort to freeze his organs to preserve them in the rare event he woke up. The room temperature was kept in the fifties. It felt even colder as air seeped out of the ice packs covering his six-foot frame. It was a new technique and the first time the nurse had tried it.

"Great—an experiment," I thought.

I discovered holding the coffee the silver-haired volunteers made each morning in my free hand while holding his frozen, swollen hand in the other kept my teeth from chattering. My human self was breaking into pieces, yet something else was happening too, and it was so strange, I could not find the words to describe it.

After the first week or so, I felt an energy building at the base of my spine. The electric current it produced began to fill up my womb and pulsate up into my stomach area. It wasn't so much in the physical body as it was active in the lower center region of my energetic body.

I didn't have the vocabulary to explain it or the knowledge to make any sense of it. I didn't have the time to research it because I was focused on my father and his current state. Later, I realized it was my soul or spirit returning to the physical body, yet at the time, all I knew was something major was happening inside of me.

I stayed sober during the day, both to witness what was going on inside me and as a fierce advocate for my father's well-being. As soon as I went home, I self-medicated with a bottle of wine followed by an Ambien or two from my husband's prescription. I binge watched *Mad Men* until the drugs kicked in.

I woke up to an alarm at 7:00 a.m. that told me it was time to go back to the hospital. This went on for six weeks—that's 42 days, 1,008 hours, 60,480 minutes, or 3,628,800 seconds—and I felt the pain of them all. I only thought I'd only drink this much wine and take the Ambien to get past the initial shock, but it would become a habit as wave after wave swept the life I had created away. There was nothing left for me to do but watch it get drug out to sea.

And, there were brief unapologetically beautiful moments of respite. I felt a soulful sensuality in the grief. I experienced a celebration of the last time I would ever be incarnated on Earth at the same time as the beautiful soul who played the role of my dad. It was not just a "goodbye, see you next lifetime." This was it, and it was lovely and beautiful and the best human life had to offer me at the given moment.

One day, not unlike the rest, my dad squeezed my hand when I repeated for the hundred thousandth time, "Dad, if you can hear me, squeeze my hand." I squeezed back, grateful, and felt warmth return to my body. The endless summer sun poured through the room's single window. For the first time in more than three weeks, I noticed it.

"Was it September already?" I asked myself. I had to check my phone. It was the first day I even wondered about the date, thought about work or my husband, or wondered about the last time I had washed my hair.

It's strange to think I was married during this period. I slept next to my husband at night, if he was home. His work took him to all sorts of places, yet there seemed to be no difference whether he was there or not. He did his best to comfort me, make sure I was fed, and take over some of my household responsibilities. Yet there was a wall between us, and I'm not sure who built it.

The real and only comfort I found was from my dog, Oliver or Ollie, a fifty-pound goldendoodle. My dad and I had picked him up from the breeder in east Texas right before my thirtieth birthday. Ollie was, and still is, an amazing presence in my life, exuding love and joy at all times.

Several days passed before my dad opened one eye, and after several days more, he opened the other. Each morning I would rush on my drive to the hospital, optimistic for news of progress. More days passed, and he wiggled his big toes. Each day brought a small but new hope-filled movement. The sky outside continued cloudless; translucent waves radiated off the asphalt parking lot, a demonstration of the triple-digit temperatures and drought the newsmen endlessly discussed on the small television in my dad's room.

Then the day came when my dad was conscious enough for me to tell him the surgery had failed. I explained to him a hole had been cut in his throat to open the airway. He could not talk now as a result. He might not be able to talk ever again. The doctor didn't know. My dad would rather hear he was dead and landed in hell than hear he might not talk again. It was the worst thing I've ever told another human being, even worse than telling my husband I was leaving him.

My dad's life was about communicating. He was a salesman who had worked his way up to CEO. He gave speeches, mentored, and held court at the Whataburger in his retirement community or on his back patio each morning over coffee. He was Texas' best inappropriate joke teller. The man made telemarketers want to hang up, and I had signed the papers approving the tracheotomy that had left him speechless.

On my way into the hospital the next day, I stopped at Target for a dry-erase board and markers, hoping to bring some optimism and an ability to communicate. But he couldn't make words, only scribble. His eyes welled up with tears, and I was mad at myself for embarrassing him as his girlfriend stood by his side.

She was a faithful and loving partner to my dad. She showed up to the hospital each and every day to support him, and I knew she loved him. Yet when it came to making health decisions, let's just say that was my job. Instead, she did what she knew how to do—she prayed to God. God—some high-and-mighty man in heaven involved in my dad's health—it was a completely outdated, limited concept to me. Something inside me knew the choice to stay or go was my father's alone, a decision of his soul. But if prayer made her feel better, who was I to say anything?

As my father's medical power of attorney, I was there for one job—to make sure his wishes were being honored in the freezer of a hospital. I consider myself a smart person, but nothing short of a medical degree would qualify me to make the decisions I was forced to make. I felt completely overwhelmed and inadequate.

He was a "do not resuscitate," or DNR, and I had to fiercely protect his right to die. And let me tell you, it was no small task. Everyone in the hospital wanted to keep him alive at any and all costs. Then it hit me like a ton of bricks square in the identity that was the do-good, cancer research and prevention funding lobbyist.

Holy shit! Was this the kind of thing I'd spent the last five years lobbying for, sacrificing my health and time to make these drug companies and medical suppliers richer? It was something I needed to revisit later; there was too much on my plate already, so I shoved it down with the other crap I did not deal with, once again.

Eventually, my dad gained enough control of his motor skills to make fists with both hands. Still without a voice, he used the opportunity to communicate through sign language. I watched him place the thumbs of each fist together and pull them swiftly apart over and over—a high stakes game of charades.

After several wrong guesses, to which he violently shook his head no, I realized it was the motion of a plug being pulled from the socket. I realized he desperately wanted me to end his life. The discussion occurred years prior during one of our weekly lunches. He had pulled out a red binder containing his will and medical power of attorney.

"Kill me if you have to, Lauren," he'd said. "Don't let me live like that."

My dad placed his hand on my wrist and looked into my eyes, the same gray-blue eyes as mine. Soul family. Lifetimes and lifetimes together. I nodded yes.

"I'll take you out," I'd said, and we'd laughed together. "I promise."

I played out the situation in my imagination. I would rip out all the cords hooked up to his body, unplug every machine, and wheel him outside into the hospital parking lot, where he could die looking into the sunlight in the triple-digit temperatures, not in this horrible, cold place.

Then I saw myself in a jail cell. The situation was ridiculous. He was ready to go. It was illegal to help him die with dignity and sovereignty, yet perfectly legal to pump him full of drugs and hook him up to machines against his will. What kind of world did we live in, what kind of world was I promoting in my career?

With nothing to do, I crawled into his hospital bed, with all the tubes and monitors, and wrapped my arms around him the best I could. We lay in silence. I cried hard and tried to keep the sobs from ringing out.

"I want a second opinion," I told the nurse the next day. "I want to hear from another pulmonologist. I want to get his regular cardiologist in here."

The shock wore off. I saw red. We were not a priority here.

"This is the only pulmonologist with privileges in this hospital," she said. "You'd have to hire an ambulance to transfer him elsewhere, and he'll never make it."

"Screw purgatory," I replied to no one in particular. "We're stuck in hell."

There are more politics in a hospital than in the fucking Texas State capitol.

Each day his girlfriend and I waited for the doctor to make his rounds, and I got angrier and angrier with him. Some days he never came, or a substitute doctor was sent who knew nothing, and then I filled them in on the state of my dad's health crisis. I sat in the arctic hospital room, a rabid advocate for the best treatment for my dad, until the sun went down and the nurses asked me to leave when visitor hours ended at 8:00 p.m.

Yet through some miracle and with the help of a small group of amazing nurses, my dad got better. His tenacious will proved stronger than his illness, likely fueled by the desire to die at home with dignity rather than in this gray, depressing, maddening hospital with no answers. He harnessed his great might and spoke his first words.

"Get. Me. Out," he gasped, finger over the hole in the tracheotomy tube protruding from his throat. He followed it up with a dramatic gesture, mimicking a racecar driver making his final left turn. The relief at hearing him speak again after so many weeks of silence rapidly turned into sorrow at seeing him in so much pain, with so much fear.

But we couldn't leave yet. The man who was so fiercely independent now could not walk or even hold himself up to go to the bathroom, so we headed to the third floor for rehab, thankful to be out of the waiting room of death and thankful he had his voice back for the time being.

When my dad was released from the rehab floor in two rather than the prescribed four to six weeks, the nurses were surprised. I was not. When I was sixteen, I'd seen him do it before when he was a lot sicker. My mom and dad had still been married at the time, and the decisions that kept me up at night were hers. I held a new respect for what she'd gone through. Taking care of a sick husband and a cocaine-addicted teenage daughter was no way to live.

My mother was forced to raise her youngest brother at age fourteen. No wonder she had left us both when my dad got well and I got sober; she had to save herself. I get that now in a way I never did before everything changed, and I'd be forced to do it myself in two years' time.

After this last resurrection, my dad went back to holding court at the Georgetown Whataburger, albeit he was slower moving and thinking. I dove back into my job headfirst. No drugs, no problem. Work addictions are much more socially acceptable and even highly encouraged in our current global economic conditions.

By this time, it was October 2011. Two months had passed. I forgot all about the soul experiences I'd gone through while my father had been in the coma. Human amnesia[13] is a real bitch.

That's when my husband received his call. Doctors had diagnosed his mother, whom I loved deeply, with stage-four colon cancer. She said there was no cure and nothing to do but try to slow it down.

Shortly thereafter, we got a call from our fertility-treatment nurse. Despite pumping myself full of hormones and being artificially inseminated, I was not pregnant, again. He was upset. I felt a huge wave of relief and then guilt for feeling the relief. After all, I'd told him I would have children with him when I'd accepted his marriage proposal. But things were different now. Everything would be different when my father died. I didn't know much, but I knew I needed to wait to see. There was absolutely no way I could be a mom right now.

I remember I did not have the energy to put up a Christmas tree the following winter, something I usually did with gusto. I wrapped a string of white lights around a rosemary bush I'd purchased on sale at the grocery store, opened a bottle of wine, put my feet up, and called it a day.

On New Year's Eve, I leaned into my husband's chest and whispered so our dinner party guests could not hear, "Surely 2012 is going to be a better year; it can't get worse." He hugged me tightly but didn't say anything.

The next call came from my mom.

"I have breast cancer," she said. "But they caught it early. No need to worry."

I was relieved to hear the doctor had caught it early. With complete removal, my mom could avoid radiation and chemo, which she said were poison. I agreed.

A couple of weeks later, my dad called in tears. His stepson had died unexpectedly in his sleep. He was in his forties and had multiple sclerosis

---

[13] The expansion and constriction, which occurs when going from an expanded soul experience back into the limited human soap opera role, without remembering you had the soul experience at all.

but was seemingly getting better with a different cocktail of medications. He and my dad were close, and his girlfriend who was now his wife, was beside herself with grief.

My dad worked way too hard for someone that sick to put his stepson's affairs in order and physically clean out his apartment. In hindsight, I think he came back from his near grave just to clean up the mess and support her before it all became too much.

Then in April, my dad told me he'd have to have another surgery. This time he was going to try something else to help with the scar tissue in his throat and remove the tracheotomy tube. He looked absolutely terrible; his skin was the color of death, and he smelled like it too. In my gut, I knew it was the end.

The surgery was experimental, but he told me he could not live with the tracheotomy tube one more day. I wanted to protest, to argue with him, but then I looked into his eyes. I knew without doubt there was no changing his mind; he saw this as his way out. He either wanted death or to get better.

The tracheotomy hole in his throat represented purgatory, and I forced myself to respect the decision. He told me over our usual weekly lunch, and when I hugged him in the parking lot, I lingered, knowing it was probably the last time I would. It was.

At lunch, my dad told me he was satisfied with his life. He loved running a company and especially loved all the people he worked with and his hundreds of friends. His regret was he did not take the time to travel when he had been healthy.

"Don't do it," he said to me. "You're on the same path."

He was right. I worked entirely too much. I promised I'd make more time for fun and travel. I had no idea what lay ahead of me was so much grander, and neither my father nor I knew we would be able to experience it together, after he was gone.

My dad's surgery was scheduled for three days before my mom's double mastectomy—in different cities. I was forced to choose where to go and who to support and attend a couple work strategy meetings in between. My dad insisted I not attend his surgery.

"You will not," he said. "You take care of your mom."

My dad came through the surgery fine and was discharged the same day. I talked with him on the phone, and he sounded ecstatic, so I ignored the feeling in my gut to go to him instead.

After my mom was wheeled into surgery, I checked my phone. Seven missed calls from my dad's house. I called back in a panic. My dad's brand-new wife handed the phone to a neighbor at the house. She couldn't even tell me herself. Bitch.

"Lauren, your dad died," said the minister's wife, flatly. "He was sitting in his chair and didn't wake up. I'm sorry."

I doubled over in grief in the hospital parking lot, yelling, "Fuck," and, "I knew it," over and over again to the minister's wife. I did not give a damn who I was yelling at.

When I see it now it's like I'm watching myself in a slow-motion movie. I see myself walk back into the hospital waiting room. I see myself tell my mom's boyfriend at the time, "My dad died. I have to go."

I see myself walk back to my car. I was not in my body. It hurt too much to be in my body. I called my husband. He did not answer, instead immediately texting me.

"In a meeting. What do you want?"

Did he not remember I was juggling two sick parents alone?

"My dad died," I texted back.

"Fuck you," I yelled to no one in particular.

The movie continued in slow motion. Was this man really my husband and texting me at a time like this? I was as work obsessed as him, I reminded myself. From outside my body, I told it we did not have energy to be mad right now. We needed to drive four hours to get to my dad's body.

I'm not sure why I was in a rush. He was dead, but it wasn't even an option not to go right that minute. The decisions we are forced to make in life are inconceivable. The things we worry about are trivial in the face of what happens out of our control.

"I should have been there for him. I should have been there when he died."

The thoughts repeated over and over. I'd sat by his deathbed off and on for sixteen fucking years, and I was not there when he fucking died. I hated myself.

My husband was smart enough to call my longtime best friend, Teresa. She talked me through the drive, telling me funny stories, keeping me occupied, and, most importantly, keeping me from driving my Infiniti G35 into the concrete highway divider at top speed. The love and appreciation I have for her—there are no words for soul friendships.

After my father died, his body was immediately taken to the funeral home for cremation. My dad thought caskets were a waste of money. I pulled out the infamous red binder, which now lived in my car, and turned to the funeral tab. I found a blank page. It included a will, a medical and financial power of attorney, a list of all bank accounts, all the bills I needed to pay, a life insurance policy, and details I didn't even know I needed. But for a funeral—the pages ran blank and my stomach dropped.

With no direction, I simply did my best to honor his life. I planned a service in the community where my father had spent his last five years. Dozens of people showed up to pay their respects. A front row of seats was reserved for family. It sat empty except for the wife who couldn't tell me my dad died, my husband who texted me to learn of my father's death, one girlfriend, my uncle's ex-wife, and me. That's it. I was full on in the soap opera that is human life.

I relied on neighbors and friends of my fathers to pull it off. I can't even remember their names now, but I am extremely grateful for the strangers who reserved rooms, helped order food, and kept things running while I was falling apart.

I gave a short speech, and when I got back home, I chased the grief I'd swallowed with a yet another bottle of wine and an Ambien. More *Mad Men* binge watching. Thank you, Don Draper.

Later in the week, I held a happy hour—much more my father's style— in Houston, where he had run a company. One hundred or so of his rowdy friends showed up, telling crazy, wild stories about my father. They drank and ate so much; the bar tab was around six thousand dollars when we were done.

It's the best money I've ever spent. I heard stories about my dad and his wild adventures I had never heard before, and the joyful mood of the crowd was so fitting for the boisterous man he was.

After a week off of work, I was expected to go back to regular life. What a fucking joke. I couldn't fathom going back to the same life. I was an entirely different person. About that time, a seemingly random and substantial check from an old family investment arrived in the mail addressed only to me.

"This is your ticket out. Go," Sar'h said energetically. "Go now."

The communication from my soul voice came from within this time. After years of patience, Sar'h itched to get back on our soul path. I told her it might take some time to untangle myself from this mess. But in the end the inevitable and natural soul progression unfolded and my human self finally got out of the damn way.

I quit my job in September, four months after my father's death. I told my husband I was not sure I could be married in October, and packed my bags for India in November. The strangest thing of all is none of this seems a big of a deal to me now—not even my father's death. They were simple human-life details that did not matter much in the context of the expansive journey of the soul—but in that moment, I was pounded by one wave after another.

Waves don't happen in singles. They roll unforgivingly in sets, growing in power and speed. I was only able to capture a few shallow breaths before the next wave punched me back down to the ocean floor. I needed more oxygen, more space, to save myself or I was going to drown. My survival came signed, sealed, and delivered in the childhood memory of the I Exist. The I Exist was my surfboard. If I could find a way to get back onto the eight-foot-six board, paddle hard into the next wave, and pop to my feet, I could ride the wave into shore. I could wake up from this strange dream turned nightmare.

In all this mess, my soul seeped back into the shell of a human I had become, into the cracks created by the shattering grief. The more my soul seeped in, the more my human life unraveled, and I found—much to my surprise—I did not want to put it back together. Something greater was bubbling up under the surface, yet I could not find the words to describe it. Could it be the self-realization or enlightenment experience I had been so quick to discard in my teens was a real possibility? It was too soon to tell.

Perhaps my journey to India would provide some much-needed insight. It would at least provide the time and space needed to figure out what was next. Regular yoga classes served as my sanctuary throughout all this. The yoga studio was the safe space to allow my emotions to flow, let myself unravel, and pull myself back together. I reasoned a month on my yoga mat at the source of the practice would afford me some answers. It was worth a try. It was all I could muster to do at the time.

6 THE VIBRATING ISLAND

NOVEMBER—DECEMBER 2012
KERALA, INDIA

Sure, I had traveled a lot before but never in search of answers to questions I could not yet articulate. It was mid-November 2012, six months after my father's death and six months before I filed for divorce. I quit working at the nonprofit about two months earlier and was still detoxing from the incessant smart phone-checking addiction it had created.

My human self was a hot mess. Sar'h was beside herself with excitement. Together we were on the verge of something so grand, my human self could not have imagined it.

Before my journey to India, I realized I was not in connection with my soul the way I had been as a child. It was going to take years to get back. I needed to relearn Mortimer and Merlyn's universal picture language and Sar'h's way of communicating in energetic sensations.

All those years in university classrooms, newsrooms, capitol buildings, and office cubicles beat my soul's voice to a pulp. Human thoughts and emotions are like muscles, gaining strength the more you use them. After the last fifteen years, it was near impossible to silence the beasts. As a child, it had been as simple as turning a light switch off and on.

Despite my efforts, I couldn't remember shit about communicating in images and sensations. The amnesia created by the density, duality, and linearity of physical Earth and non-stop human thoughts and subsequent emotions created a situation in which my soul experiences felt like a thousand-piece puzzle I must put back together.

Yet, it certainly wouldn't be boring, I reasoned. My human expression hated being bored. Besides, there was no going back. If I tried to stay in the singular human experience, I would die like a houseplant no one watered. My human expression, some call ego, panicked and tried to understand what was occurring. Yet the more it tried to comprehend through limited human thoughts and emotions, the more internal knots it created.

The only thing to do was relax—to *allow*—but true relaxation is not the human's forte. The human brain wants goals, plans, security, answers, and rigid categories to keep messy things like emotions organized. Experiences of the soul? Forget it. Total brain malfunction. The soul, the I Exist—all of it is beyond comprehension of a human brain's local linear thought patterns.

On a human level, the most pressing matter I had to decide was if I was going to stay in my marriage or not. The thing is, I knew deep down, at the soul level, I was going to leave. Yet my human thoughts—the kind that skip like broken records and keep you awake at night—and my husband's incessant yelling and crying were so loud, it was near impossible to hear the inner voice. At the time, all I knew was I needed to exit my current hurricane of a situation to be able to view it from an expanded perspective.

Then the opportunity arose. A friend of mine and another yoga teacher were hosting yoga teacher training on a tiny island in the Vembanad backwaters of Kerala, India.

Please note the irony of two white American women hosting yoga teacher training—in India of all places—was not lost on me. However, it was at the time a husband-approved and socially acceptable way for me to find peace for a month, get sober, and hopefully dig some more clues out of my soul and reconnect to the experiences of expanded awareness I had had as a child and a teenager.

The Rumi poem about the lost camel came to mind: "You have lost your camel, my friend. And all around you people are full of advice. You don't know where your camel is. But you do know that these casual directions are wrong."

I was off to look for my camel, and somehow or another I knew the compass, the north star of knowingness was not something to seek outside of myself, but rather it lay in wait inside of me. These people who showed up in the chaos to point me in the so-called right direction seemed more lost than me. No more seeking an outside authority — it didn't work in the human reality and it was not going to work in the spiritual one either.

Yoga came barreling into my life in 2006. I was a total stress ball, attending graduate school and teaching indoor-cycling and weight lifting classes at 24 Hour Fitness on the side. I was completely and totally body obsessed. I tallied how many calories I expended and ingested the way an obsessive person washes his or her hands and checks to make sure a door is locked.

Injured and over-exercised, I found myself in the yoga studio by my home. The instructor talked me into pigeon pose, which was no fun for me at the time. Yet something strange happened as I eased my body forward into the deep hip-opening stretch. I began to cry, not from pain but from an almost orgasmic emotional release. It was if I had stored a giant knot inside my emotion hip body decades, if not lifetimes, ago, and I finally let whatever it was go, and untie itself. After the experience, I was hooked, reading everything I could get my hands on and practicing as much as possible.

"Welcome aboard Emirates flight 1304 Dallas to Dubai. The estimated flight time is fifteen hours and twenty-five minutes," the captain said. His voice boomed from the overhead speaker as he read the flight message in English, Arabic, and something I did not recognize.

"Hi, I'm Mark," said the man in the window seat. "This is Bill, my father-in-law."

He gestured to the man who sat between us.

"I'm Lauren. Where are you headed?" I asked to be polite. He clearly wanted to tell me.

"To Mumbai for a mission trip," Mark said.

"Good luck with that," I thought.

"We're all from Oklahoma City," he said.

Bill gestured to five men who sat in the middle section one row up and named their mutual church. I couldn't tell if it was Baptist or Church of Christ, but I didn't care enough to ask.

"Where are you going?" Mark asked.

"To an island in Kerala to practice yoga for a month."

"By yourself?"

"Well, I'm meeting some friends there, but yes."

Then it occurred to me their group included no women. They must have stayed home to tend to the children back in Oklahoma, where morality was safe. They existed on a different plane of reality perception— one where you held onto traditions of the past for dear life.

This marks the space when—as an adult—I begin to understand Earth realities were fragmenting into thousands of different experiences. Some talk of new Earth and old Earth, but I saw so clearly thousands of Earth realities to choose from.

The difference—these people never saw with any awareness a choice existed. This was the only reality they knew, the only play to choose from— one life resulting in heaven or hell finality. A script as old as time.

When the plane leveled in the air, the attendant made her rounds. Her crimson pillbox hat and tailored suit were a far cry from the sweatshop uniforms American attendants wear. She was young, beautiful, and appeared to be from the entire continent of Asia.

"Ma'am, what would you like to drink?"

"Two Bloody Mary's, please."

I needed one for each Ambien. I wanted the wheels of the plane hitting Dubai concrete to wake me up. I certainly did not want to spend fifteen hours brooding over the mess I had left in Texas.

"Also, please don't wake me up for food. I just ate a huge meal and will be fine."

"As you wish, ma'am."

The two men looked at me in horror as I opened the tiny vodka bottles and dumped the entire contents into the bland tomato juice and seasoned them with the tiny packets of pepper. I downed them back-to-back for the sake of show. I was snoring and drooling in about twenty minutes and only remembered waking up to go to the bathroom once.

When I got off the plane, Mark and Bill confessed they hadn't slept at all. I felt like a spring daisy. "God would have wanted it that way," I chuckled to myself.

After passing through several security lines, I wound through a labyrinth lined with women covered head to toe in fabric, who tended to children and pushed carts stacked high with all their worldly belongings. They walked behind their husbands, whose hands remained free.

I located food and wine and watched movies on my computer to pass the time between flights. An hour before takeoff, I parked my backpack and single rolling suitcase at the gate, keeping my eye out for the friends who would accompany me on the next leg of the journey.

It wasn't hard to spot my friend who was the lead yoga instructor at the one-month training. Her wild, curly hair seemed bigger than normal, and I wondered how the good people of Dubai felt about a braless woman in a tank top with unshaven armpits.

She introduced her boyfriend, the one she had left her husband for, whom I had heard a lot about but had never actually met. He looked like a juggler without clubs. His floppy hat and pirate smile were friendly, and his harem pants completed the look.

They both gave me hugs, and I felt myself exhale for the first time in what seemed like months. It wasn't so much their company that relaxed me as much as the reality of finding peace for one month setting in.

I was a long way from home and the life I'd been living—one of Neiman Marcus suits, Prada heels, and lobby strategy meetings. Somehow, the funny Polaroid picture the three of us made told me I was going in the right direction. I had found a pause between the sets of breaking waves. I had time to breathe.

The four-hour connecting flight from Dubai to Port Cochin was uneventful until we landed, when the passengers emptied the plane in order of who could shove harder. I put my elbows up and shoved. Never fuck with a Texan woman.

It was surprisingly easy to get through customs and retrieve our luggage, which wasn't much for a thirty-day stay. You don't need much for practicing yoga in triple-digit temperatures; and with no audience for hair, makeup, and high heels, I was down a suitcase.

An older Indian man with a sign with the name of our destination waited as we walked outside. A damp heat slapped me hard on both cheeks, and it felt good to me compared to Texas' November chill. This man was not the cabdriver. His role was simply to point at the car we should get in, while the driver, who appeared to be no older than fourteen or fifteen, strapped our luggage to the top.

The teenager drove us through the empty streets of the dark city, veering from lane to lane wildly. Hello, India! The yoga teacher sat in the front seat, hand over her stomach, attempting not to get carsick, while her boyfriend told me about his sun sign. I pretended to listen.

"Sagittarius," I mumbled in response as I rolled down the window, allowing the thick, humid breeze in. I sensed the energetic feel of the country. It was the first Eastern country I had been to, yet it felt unexpectedly familiar.

A memory surfaced like the one I'd experienced holding the book of King Arthur and Merlyn in my thirteen-year-old hands. I saw a figure I knew was my dad. I was a small child, and he was telling me stories about studying in India. He described the long journey he took to get there from his home miles and miles away. I realized it was Sar'h's memory of another lifetime, not Lauren's. Or were they one and the same?

Previous lives were beginning to run simultaneously, one leaking into the other. It made sense at the soul level. If time were not linear, how else would they run but simultaneous? It confused my human self beyond its limits of comprehension, creating another residual knot inside of me.

About an hour later, we came to a tall iron gate, and two guards opened each side enough to allow the tiny car to pull through. The gate shut immediately with a thud that felt like the nail on the coffin of my self-induced, month-long sobriety. The dark curtain of the night began to lift, but the sun was not yet visible.

We climbed aboard a small boat, and yet another Indian man loaded our luggage. A thatched roof covered one side of the boat, which was made of wood and featured a basic motor slapped on the back. Another Indian man drove the boat, and yet another guided at the front with a flashlight. He used a long spear to move the copious lily pads covering the surface out of the way, and I noticed he was careful not to damage them.

As we approached the island, the hum of the tiny engine combined with the chorus of what must have been thousands and thousands of birds. Daylight approached, and I stood awestruck as the thick, tangled, flower-blooming lily pads coating the lake moved in unison with the current.

The sun broke with the coconut tree line into the curried sky. If I had not known it was the same sun, I might have sworn it was different. I looked at my travel companions to confirm I was there and this was not a dream. I could see them memorizing the colors and lines of the horizon like me, perhaps to tuck the image away for future gray days.

The entire staff of the island, which at one time had served as a hospital and now served as a refuge for the overworked and untreatable by

Western medicine, seemed to be waiting on our arrival. Gold, merengue, and saffron flower petals covered the grand entrance where we stepped off the boat.

I reached for my luggage, but a young Indian man beat me to it. Another man who looked to be about forty years old introduced himself as Babu, and you could tell he was in charge because he was the only one in Western clothing.

His lilac button-down shirt was tucked into heavily starched eggplant slacks, belt drawn tightly around his thick middle. The women wore saris in various jewel tones, and the men wore loose, white linen pants and kurtas made of the same material on top.

Babu rattled over the basics, and his head bobbled when we asked questions. I was unable to tell if the head bobble meant yes or no, and later I would learn it meant both or neither and a question was just a way to declare what you wanted and they would try to make it happen, God willing. It was the Indian version of the Arab world's *inshallah* and was just as reliable.

A skinny, attractive young man named Salu struggled with my luggage as he led the way to my room. On the way, we passed a hissing fountain with three blooming white lotus flowers. It was the first time I had seen them in person, and I noticed they appeared to be growing from a pond of muck, which smelled strongly of shit.

The combination of the birds, insects, and chanting from a neighboring village made the island feel as if it were vibrating under my feet, like the vibration kept it afloat—and if it were to stop, the whole island, perhaps the whole country of India would sink into oblivion, maybe taking the rest of the world with it.

I drug my jet-lagged, somewhat drunk, and somewhat hungover body up a spiral, narrow iron staircase. Behind me, Salu panted while dragging my forty-eight-pound suitcase, two pounds below the airline limit. There was a bed with stark white sheets, an antique armoire the same color of the rich wood floors, and a bathroom covered in tiny sea-foam-green tiles.

I handed him a five-dollar bill, and he smiled so big, he showed the bottom row of his white teeth. His head bobbled furiously, and it occurred to me I'd likely just paid him a month's salary. I witnessed a thought form through the look in his eyes, and he autocorrected to Western speak and manner. He worked to hold his head steady and said slowly, "Thank you, ma'am. Please let me know if you need anything."

"Please call me Lauren," I said and smiled. He seemed to loosen up a bit.

I quickly traded my travel clothes for my yoga clothes and joined the eleven people who were already deep into their morning practice just below my balcony. The yoga *shala* was a concrete slab with a thatched roof.

Bamboo blinds hung from three sides of the rectangle and served as a playground for the many lizards that flipped and twisted up and down the rungs.

I unrolled my mat and joined in the middle of the practice. I exhaled through *chaturanga dandasana*, inhaled into *urdhva mukha svanasana* (upward-facing dog), and exhaled into *adho mukha svanasana* (downward-facing dog), completing my first *vinyasa*.

On the last and seventy-second *vinyasa* in the practice, I surrendered to where I was and made peace with what I was here to experience. I lay in *savasana*, the ending relaxation pose, raw and unguarded. The critical human brain flexed its well-developed muscles. I wondered if I'd be able to make the thirty days.

I didn't have to worry much about anything. It was all laid out for me. Wake up at 5:45 a.m. and silently make my way to the yoga mat in the moonlight. Practice the *ashtanga* primary series, an ancient Indian *asana* (physical yoga practice), which takes about ninety minutes to complete.

Follow it up with a thirty-minute *pranayama*, or breathing, practice. Finally, meditate. Make my way silently back to my room to shower, and hand-wash the yoga clothes now drenched in sweat. Dress in loose-fitting yoga clothes, braid my hair, and slide into the flip-flops resting outside my door.

Finally, at 9:00 a.m. there was breakfast—a major event. I started off with freshly squeezed mango juice and two eggs from the neighboring village. A buffet was set up with pancake-like breads, stewed okra with indescribable spices, and a freshly baked fruitcake nothing like the Christmas variety back home. I finished it off with a pot of coffee and hot lemon ginger water for digestion over conversation with the eleven other students who represented six different countries.

Next, the twelve of us would move back to the outdoor practice area and pull up a chair for theory. In these sessions, we voraciously memorized everything we could so we could regurgitate it in a written exam, which would be graded along with our ability to teach a yoga class at the month's end. Yes, it felt a bit ridiculous, but it was actually lovely to give my brain something to do while my soul began to seep back into my body.

Because I had denied the soul for so long, basically operating as a human shell by walking around with no inner guidance and governed completely by external expectations and societal norms, it felt foreign as the soul began to return.

It could be painful at times, creating a dull cringe-worthy ache over my entire body. My feet hurt especially. The nerve endings felt like live wires. As these physiological changes were occurring, I began to witness almost everyone denied the existence of his or her soul too. I could see their souls hovering outside their bodies on many occasions.

An Episcopalian priest named John A. Sanford said it quite well in his book *The Kingdom Within: The Inner Meaning of Jesus' Sayings*. In it, Sanford states,

"The soul today is an orphan. Her ancient parents have abandoned her; she languishes alone and forsaken in a rationalistic world that no longer believes in her. Philosophy, her father, long decided she did not exist and cast her aside. He hardly noticed that in doing so he turned himself away from the pursuit of wisdom…The church, her mother, fell unwittingly into the clutches of the extraverted, rationalistic materialism of our times and so she also abandoned the soul; she did not notice that in losing the soul she lost her ability to relate the individual to God."[14]

I'd argue the soul is also missing from modern-day spirituality. In all my three hundred hours of yoga teacher training, two hundred in India and another one hundred in Peru a year later, I never heard the mention of soul even once.

Instead, I learned why eating *tamasic* foods like mushrooms, onions, and meat was bad for your spirituality. Every single bit of information on the chakras was covered. Yet when living in alignment with the soul, all the chakras align into one. There is no separation. There is but one chakra—the I Exist.

Like everyone around me, I had read all the books on mindfulness, brain-focused meditation techniques, the law of attraction, and heart-centered living, but again, the soul remained the orphan.

Everyone else could sit around trying to make their limited human brain work better, to control their emotions and perfect their bodies. I, on the other hand, was headed to the orphanage to pick my soul up—bust her out of that joint. I knew better than to share that bit of information with anyone around me. I found myself back in the third-grade classroom, angry as ever, but I would not make the mistake of oversharing again.

In the training, we learned *ashtanga* translated directly from Sanskrit to mean "eight limbs," which served as guidelines for living. Patanjali, a sage who lived sometime between 200 and 500 BCE, laid out these tenants in a text called the *Yoga Sutras*. The eight limbs run in order of accomplishment. *More linear crap to digest. Nothing conscious ever comes in a list. Write that down.*

They started with the *yamas*, which are universal practices dealing with one's ethical standards and sense of integrity, such as nonharming and nonstealing. Basically, it's the Ten Commandments—Patanjali style. *Niyama*, the second limb, covers self-discipline and spiritual observances, much like saying grace before meals or taking contemplative walks alone.

I've never been the biggest fan of goals or disciplining the human

---

[14] Sanford, John A. *The Kingdom Within: The Inner Meaning of Jesus' Sayings*. San Francisco: Harper San Francisco, 1987.

aspect of Self. The human is never going to perfect itself no matter how spiritual it pretends to be—that's just another role to play on the human stage, another identity to discard, though, I realized most would spend many lifetimes trying to do so.

The third limb, *asana*, includes the physical postures practiced in what Westerners call yoga. The fourth limb, *pranayama*, covers techniques designed to master breath control with the recognition of the connection between the breath, mind, and emotions. Again, no mention of soul is included anywhere, just many complicated steps for breathing.

"How about inhaling and exhaling with awareness—and done?" my soul interjected.

The first four limbs cover awareness of the human part of the Self, which I'll admit is a great way to keep it busy. My problems in all this yogic and spiritual philosophy lie in the rules to control the human self, rather than the simple awareness of it. I wasn't really interested in improving my human self. The human was and is, by definition, imperfect. It ate cheeseburgers and drank too much wine. Why could we not simply let the human be human? I understood living a perfect human life was not a requirement of the self-realization process. In fact, I thought it probably wasn't possible to perfect the human. If it were possible, it would be awfully boring.

I wanted to stand up, stamp my feet, and yell, "It's the soul, stupid!"

And then I wondered why I had such strong thoughts about it. I realized my condemnation of those around me was really a condemnation of myself. I was mad at myself for taking so long to recognize the soul voice, the God within me. I realized everyone around me was going through a soul evolution too, but the words were not spoken out loud. I knew I wouldn't be ready to share or teach anything before I moved beyond the desire to condemn.

My human self, what some call ego, was still playing too much of a role in everything in my life. Keeping silent was the best choice. Because I could not ask the question aloud, I asked Sar'h internally, "What is the soul, anyway?"

When I sensed into it, I received my answer—the soul is the part of us that does not change from lifetime to lifetime or in between lives. It is the wise being within our human physical form that retains information, or wisdom, rather, from any and all experiences throughout the soul's existence. This wisdom the soul retained from all lifetimes and in between lives was available to the current human expression of Self at any time.

"That's how you know the language of images and sensations," Sar'h said to me energetically. "You learned it well before coming into this life. To remember you only need to connect with that understanding."

I flashed back to the long conversations I'd had with Mortimer in the backyard garden of my childhood home. In this moment of openness, it became overwhelmingly clear to me. It was not some external God or the universe we were seeking, but the God living within all of us—what lay beneath our "turtle shells."

Every human, myself included, wanted to grab at something external for answers. Yet the intense craving for external answers and support from above was really a deep desire to get to know the God inside all of us—the soul—a desire to experience our inner divinity, to know that at the soul level we are God, too.

It's what Yeshua, or Jesus, meant when he said the kingdom is within; he was here to show us how to find the Christ within ourselves, not be worshipped as a guru or worse, a twisted religious icon.

Because of my Catholic upbringing, I understood why the notion of understanding I was, in fact, God too was blasphemous in religious communities—that was a given—but wondered how it had become taboo in spiritual, New Age, and yogic communities.

How could one be 'woke' without seeing, sensing, and knowing their inner divinity? Didn't *namaste* mean the God in me recognizes the God in you? It seemed to me *namaste* was about honoring one another at the soul level; it was the recognition of the GodSelves living within all of us.

And if they did recognize the soul's true creator nature, why did they continue to deny it by constantly referencing this universe character as the creator or co-creator of their reality? It seemed to me the universe replaced the religious God in the modern spiritual conversation. It held the same status as a wiser, external being, which existed to guide you from outside yourself.

Anytime someone said "the universe," I realized it could be replaced with "God," holding the same concept. The people around me were incessantly looking for signs from the universe (God). They prayed to the universe (God) for external guidance and yelled at the universe (God) when their lives did not go according to their human plans.

In my realizations, I teetered on the tip of awareness my soul, my spirit, could completely embody human form, which I sensed was a form of mastery in and of itself, before quickly falling back into the limits of my human awareness.

The moments of clarity tended to quickly fade, giving way to the heavy human thoughts and emotions consuming me at the time. Like the lotus flowers in the hissing fountain, the shelf life of the bloom was short, and then I closed back up again, returning to the muck from which my human expression came.

In our lessons, I was told the fifth through eighth limb dealt with attaining a higher state of consciousness, and my ears perked up. Yes, this is what called to me in this yogic experience, not all these rules governing the human, the quest for a perfect handstand, and especially not the perfect yogi diet.

Instead, the teachers, who had no direct experience climbing those tree limbs, glossed over textbook definitions we were expected to memorize for the test. I was read the following.

Pratyahara, the fifth limb, is an effort to draw awareness away from the external world and direct attention internally. Okay, now we're talking. Internal, that's where my soul voice resided. The sixth limb, *dharana*, is the ability to concentrate on a single point, and the seventh limb, *dhyana*, is meditation or being keenly aware without focus.

Aware without focus—that sounds and feels a lot like consciousness, which can only be done when we move beyond the limits of the human mind and its emotions. It was getting better. Finally, *samadhi*, the eighth limb, is the ultimate goal. Patanjali describes this final stage of *ashtanga* as a state of ecstasy. At this stage, the meditator transcends the self completely and comes to realize a profound interconnectedness with all living things.

More so than interconnectedness, which I had felt so deeply as a child, in India I was sensing my sovereignty, the self-governing nature of the soul, the soul's ability to solely create its reality without the interference of an external God or the universe—or as the boy King Arthur learns, authority over Self.

I understood deeply recognizing the sovereign nature of the soul was synonymous with recognizing we are the creators of our reality, not God or the universe character everyone around me was so intent to reference.

We spent about ten minutes tops on this, and as a greater reflection of the American yogic community, it was implied these stages were limited to holy men who sat in caves in Nepal and mountains in Tibet.

Bullshit. It was the same limits I had hit in book, *The 21 Lessons of Merlyn*. I realized the teachers had lost their camels too, so I went inside for answers.

The whisper was faint, but it didn't waver. It said once again Self-mastery, or realization, was available to me in this lifetime, to hundreds—maybe even thousands—of others who were coming to the end of their human experiences as well.

I wouldn't dare say it out loud because it would be enough to have me completely kicked out of the figurative yogi village, and at the time my human still cared about appearances and fitting in.

Yet as the seed of my soul began to sprout through the cracks the grief had created, I knew one thing for sure—if I chose to experience it, self-realization was available to me in this lifetime. I had not made it up as a teen. I was not a faker or a pretender. It was not some crazy childhood dream. I knew this life, if I chose it, held potentials for grandness—if I could move beyond all the noise and distractions.

I thought of Mortimer and what he'd told me. Was I really here on Earth to share some sort of truths or wisdom? If so, I knew there were others too. Where were they? Could I allow my human self to believe Mortimer, to trust Sar'h? Was that completely insane? Sar'h's voice was buried deep, and her language of images and sensations were still hard for me to decipher, but I found if I became really still and deeply allowed myself to open to it, the voice would come through clearly.

"Sar'h, was Mortimer right?" I asked. "Do I contain these truths?"

"Only if you have the will and the courage needed to peel back all the layers that buried them," she replied. I didn't know my answer.

Was I willing to change my relationship with the human experience in order to experience the path of the soul in human form? I realized I stood at the crossroads once again.

At age eight and again at age sixteen, I had chosen to drop the soul off at the orphanage, trading her for a normal human life. Would I do it again? Staying in my marriage was saying good-bye to my soul for as long as it lasted; leaving would allow her to return. It was a decision I did not take lightly.

As quickly as the conversation of clarity occurred within me, my human self shoved it back down into the depths where uncomfortable things are hidden. My human yelled, "Focus! Our security is being threatened! What are you going to do? Get a divorce? Stay married and suffer for the sake of security and propriety? How are you going to make money? Don't you know that's just ego talking about all this enlightenment stuff? Give me a break."

Wah-wah. Wah-wah. My brain was beginning to sound like the teacher in a Charlie Brown cartoon.

Post—theory lessons, we'd break for a dip in the pool and have lunch, which was equally as spectacular as breakfast. Then we'd try to keep our eyes open in the afternoon heat while we learned to teach each posture in the *ashtanga* primary series. I'll admit it: I loved this part. Being in a human body can be a killer experience. Feeling it twist and turn into yoga postures was and is a real joy for me, and for Sar'h too.

Next, we'd practice teaching and adjusting postures on our fellow students and finish up just in time for meditation, which was followed by dinner, the grand food finale for the day.

It often left the group clapping and cheering for the kitchen staff. Finally, we'd chant, meditate, sing *kirtan*, or watch a video before drifting off to sleep in our private bungalows to the vibration of the night's nocturnal birds, including a large owl family.

Meals were not only for sharing food but also for sharing stories, and I love a good story. What Texan doesn't? I learned early on I was not the only one on the vibrating island in major conflict or experiencing tidal wave-level grief.

One of the teachers was also painstakingly deciding whether to work on or walk out of a marriage. Another's boyfriend had recently died from cancer in his late twenties. That woman and I shared the pain only someone can comprehend when his or her best friend in the world has left a physical body. The stories went on from everyone around me and weighed so heavily upon me I remember waking up one morning and writing down in my journal in big, bold letters—TO SUFFER IS HUMAN—and I felt it all so intensely.

Suddenly, I was back in junior high, absorbing the energies around me, but somehow it was starting to feel different. I realized if I expanded from the I Exist, the fixed point within my body of consciousness, and made my energetic field larger in every direction, I would not absorb others' emotions and experiences at such a rate.

In this expanded state, I realized I could choose to observe rather than engage. Conversely, I realized instead of receiving input from my environment, I could sit in the I Exist, while also being in human awareness simultaneously, but I could not hold it for long.

At this time, the realizations would come in quick moments of clarity, which were often followed by the muddled and muted experience of the human. I was starting to notice a pattern.

As soon as I experienced a soul realization, my human brain would jump in to discredit it with logic and reason almost immediately. As my human voice came in, it would twist the soul experience into a story, often strangling the soul's wisdom beyond recognition. It was a confusing time, and with all this internal dialogue, I probably appeared a little bizarre to my new friends.

But it wasn't all suffering. My new friends knew how to laugh and celebrate too. On the evening of November 27, 2012, my thirty-second birthday and the first since losing my father, I was surprised with an American-style chocolate cake that read Happy Birthday in pink icing.

As the Indian kitchen crew presented it, the candles lining the tables beneath the coconut grove illuminated their bright white teeth, which formed giant goofy grins in genuine celebration of me. Their head bobbles of joy seemed to vibrate in unison with the island, and I knew they'd gone to great lengths to get this cake to our tiny, remote island.

My new friends sang happy birthday to me as Salu lit the single candle on the cake. A plastic lotus flower began to spin, opening its petals. Once it stopped, I made my wish for clarity in decision and blew the candle out.

Tears of gratitude for the overwhelming love and support poured down my face. I was happy to receive and absorb all the energies of the moment. It was a birthday I will never forget. In so much pain and suffering there is always a silver lining, and for me, the most treasured experience in all of my human existence is friendship. I don't think there is any purer form of human love than the loose love of a good friend.

I pulled the plastic lotus from the cake, and in true vibrating-island fashion, we all stuffed our faces so much, it took ten pots of lemon ginger tea to digest it. I went to bed that night with a full belly and a full heart. I would wake up to a husband screaming at me on Skype the next morning, but tonight, I was thirty-two, and the world was full of love and possibilities.

When we make major decisions in life, we often search for a voice from above, for clear direction from God, a sign from the universe, from anywhere outside ourselves. The real answer is but a steady whisper from deep within we can only hear if we are still enough to listen.

Sometimes it takes a friend to translate or reflect back to us what we already know at the soul level but cannot yet see clearly. For me, that friend was a tall, thin Indian man who no longer inhabited a physical body and no one else but me could see. My merlin. Mentioning him brings tears of gratitude to my eyes.

My Indian friend appeared to me during mediation one steamy afternoon toward the end of my month-long journey. As I lay there in stillness, open to receive whatever he had to share, my right hand lit up. I was told to write through energetic sensations and images. It was the same picture language I had been fluent in as a child; it was coming back to me. My soul found this soothing; my human protested.

"Write what? What the fuck do you want me to write?"

"Your story. Write your story," the Indian whispered calmly.

"Oh, sorry."

I wouldn't know his name until October of the following year, but I sensed his presence daily. He wasn't there to give me answers. He wasn't there to give me advice. He was simply there. It's not so much he was holding space for me; rather, he was honoring my soul's journey. His presence was a reminder of why I was really here on Earth. It was not to be a wife, a mother, or career woman—all great human experiences, but they were not what I really wanted at the soul level and all were roles I have played many times before. Instead, those roles were expectations coming from outside me. That I knew. But beyond it, I could not form words. I only felt a sensation telling me more information would be revealed around the corner.

Go further. What I must do became undeniably clear. To see what was around the corner, I was going to have to untangle myself from the human life I had built in its entirety, even if it meant hurting a man I loved but could no longer live with.

"Start to come back into your body," I heard the teacher instruct at the end of the meditation. The Indian vanished, and I made my way back to my physical reality. Before I had the chance to sit up, Sar'h's voice came in clearly.

She said through images and sensations my father's death was the loose thread in the sweater that was my human life, and he had timed it perfectly before there was a child brought into this world. Instead of sewing it back into repair—and my human expression wanted to do that so badly—the voice of my soul said pull it. Pull the thread hard, and let the whole sweater unravel.

I had already walked out of my job and the identity attachment that came with it. In India, I was offered another position lobbying for another non-profit. It felt like a test. If I were going to leave my husband, this job would provide financial security.

Was I really ready to be who I actually was, or did I want to play the human game a little bit more? I turned it down, realizing choice was a sense of the soul of its own, like imagination or dreaming. Each choice we make, no matter how small, determines our reality. Choices direct us toward our mastery or to another limited human experience, yet there is no right or wrong answer. I quite liked all my past human experiences, but now I was ready to go grand.

I was going home and moving through the motions over Christmas and New Year's Day. I would honor my husband, who had been a major part of my life. We would spend our last Christmas as a family, and I would figure out how to leave somehow. I was going to appear insane and evil to everyone around me, and I had to let that go as well.

When my thirty days of sobriety, yoga, and friendship on the vibrating island were up, I hesitantly packed my bags to make the long journey home. The human part of me did not want to leave the comfort of the island's vibration, the glorious colors, the stifling heat cooled only by the milk of a machete-cut coconut, the song of the birds, and the dance of the lizards.

My soul assured me what was around the corner would be so amazing, my human imagination could not even fathom it. I shuddered to think I would never again see Salu's bright white smile greeting me each morning as he handed me the newspaper and my coffee.

I boarded the plane and ordered a beer. Funny, it didn't taste as good as I remembered. Maybe a month of yoga and meditation did not answer my questions, but it sure as hell allowed the space for me to reconnect with my soul.

Maybe I was a bit disappointed in the limits I'd hit in the yogic community, but the experienced paved the way for what lay ahead. I was grateful for the experiences the teachers had created and for the new friends

I had made as well.

I paused to stop with the collective modern-day yogi consciousness on their journey to wherever. I joke it was perhaps to the vegan, gluten-free grocery store or the statue and crystal covered alter near their one-hundred-and-fifty-dollar yoga mats.

Seriously though, I honored it, knowing I would continue to forge my own path—further into Self. This saying goodbye thing is something I did many times, and it never seemed to get easier for my human expression of Self.

And really that's why I joke so much—laughter breaks up all the stuck energy. I felt a deep love for my then-friends but also an honoring of each of their unique soul journeys, something I was beginning to see so clearly not only in myself but in everyone around me. The soul expansion was setting in, and I felt wonderfully whole.

Yet, it all came to a screeching halt when I landed back on American soil. Somehow being back in Texas sent me back into the familiar state of amnesia, in which my human self forgot all the soul clarity we had experienced on the vibrating island.

My human sank back into the drama. It took me another six months to summon the courage needed to leave my marriage and return to the path of the soul—once again.

7 THE MENU, THE CAGE, AND THE PILLS

JUNE 2012—JUNE 2013

About a month after my father died, I vividly recall sitting on a barstool drinking a cup of coffee in my home, the one my husband and I moved into on our first wedding anniversary.

My elbows were resting on the granite countertops. I looked around the room at my perfect home. Anyone I knew at the time would kill to live here, including me two years prior. I should be grateful and shut up, I told myself, but I couldn't shake the feeling I was a stranger in my own home.

It wasn't just the home that felt foreign; it was the whole life—the one I had chosen, the one I had thought I wanted to live. I walked through the long hallway of the house into the master bedroom and then through the master bathroom and into my closet.

I skimmed my fingers along all the beautiful clothes lining my closet walls. Even my clothes did not feel like they belonged to me. This was not me. None of this. Not the husband. Not the house. Not the job. I felt like a stranger in my own life.

I looked down at the diamond overwhelming my left ring finger, and I wondered, "How did I get here? Why did I choose this, and why does it feel like someone else's life? Is this not what I wanted?"

And, better yet, how was I going to get myself out of here? I was overwhelmed and terrified of the changes occurring inside me. My human stressed if we were not going to live here, married, what were we going to do? What was the plan?

I met my husband for the first time on one of the coldest nights in our Texas home. It was December 9, 2005, shortly after my twenty-fifth birthday. I was wearing cheap jeans, heels from Payless, a black shirt, and a $1.99 rainbow-striped scarf from Forever 21.

I worked as a newspaper reporter for thirteen dollars per hour after being let go from the state senator's office while waiting to see if I was accepted to graduate school. I'd covered the cheap outfit with a nice black pea coat I had purchased, a huge splurge at ninety-nine dollars on discount, for an impending trip to New York City to see a girlfriend.

When I walked into the Italian restaurant my date had chosen over e-mail, I told the hostess I was looking for my date. She pointed me in his direction, and I wove through the crowd, full of nerves.

He was sipping a glass of red wine, and I noticed a nice bottle of Pinot Noir sitting next to it. He had beautiful green eyes and dark, curly hair, just long enough to rest on the back of the collar of his cream-colored sweater. His eyes were kind and his touch gentle. He exuded the rugged good looks of a bearded REI model. I remember thinking, "Wow, he is stunning!"

We had met on an online dating site I signed up for when I had been laid off from my position as the press secretary for a state senator. That same week, I'd found out I had a cyst in my left ovary threatening to blow itself up.

As a result, I had begun to think about kids as the threat of infertility loomed. Months had passed. I went on crappy date after crappy date. This man was different. I knew instantly I had known him before—his soul, not in this body. The familiarity comforted me, and conversation flowed easily. I had not yet learned about karmic relationships.

He ordered the veal. I had the fish. We laughed and chatted while he sipped an after-meal cappuccino. At the end of the date, we walked out to his car. He hugged me respectfully and made plans quickly to see me again. We stepped on the fast track. We were seeing each other all the time, even traveling together to Spain. I moved in eight short months later, right before I started graduate school. But I knew something was off. It was a gut feeling, and it was confirmed by the voice—the same one that told me my dad would die and I would go to jail if I didn't do something soon.

One day before I moved in, we were kissing on his couch. The voice came in loud and clear once more, telling me something was very off in this relationship.

"Wow! I must really be losing my mind," I thought, and like the times before and after, I buried the words, but the voice had been clear and direct. After we had been living together for about two years, a deep feeling arose in my gut and said I needed to get out of the relationship.

I couldn't shake the feeling I was being controlled from behind the scenes. It was too intense to ignore. I tried my best to leave. Found an apartment, but he talked me back into staying, like he would the first and second times I tried to leave our marriage. Instead, his grip on me became even tighter, and he proposed to me right before Christmas in 2009 at the same restaurant where we had first met.

I said yes. This was what I was supposed to do next. That was what people did after graduate school and landing their first big job. I was supposed to get married to an attractive businessman who liked to travel, a man who would take care of me, who wanted a weekend home on the lake.

Then I was supposed to produce an heir. It fit seamlessly into the check mark on the list society had handed me when I moved out of my parents' house at the age of seventeen. He was not perfect. No one was, I told myself, and I loved him in the best way I knew how to at the time—a time when I did not even know how to love myself.

I had at least a dozen friends who cried themselves to sleep because they couldn't find a husband. When I met my future husband, I lived with a woman, six years my senior. At thirty-one, she had become the old maid. She would come home from date after date, crying, claiming, "I am never going to get married!" And the thought of turning into her terrified me. I had no idea other options existed.

We live in a world where freedom and choice are illusions. We are told we can grow up to be anything we want to be, marry whomever we want to marry. We can have anything off the menu put in front of us, but you couldn't order off the menu.

The option to not get married and to forgo children did not appear on the menu. It wasn't something you would choose; that's where you ended up if you lost the game. Those kinds of women were pitied and labeled as damaged goods. It wasn't as pronounced as it had been in the 1950s, but the taboo still existed all around me.

According to society, I was one of the lucky ones. The menu handed to me was one of a Michelin-star restaurant. Marriage afforded me the opportunity to live in an impressive cage—one I could decorate in any way I wanted to. I was given a fat diamond ring as a consolation prize and financial security.

As a wife, I felt like an attraction at the zoo, an exotic animal. It was a picture-perfect life as long as you stayed in the cage and behaved, as long as you were pretty and smart, as long as you birthed some beautiful children to seal the deal.

I know many people would gladly cut off their right pinkies to have these options. Before I had 'it all' I would have too. After being let go from the senator's office and before I found another reporting gig, I was barely scraping by on unemployment checks totaling eight hundred dollars monthly.

In that place of scarcity, I told myself if I had a partner, a savings account, vacations in exotic locals, nicer clothes, and a better career, the dull ache that whispered, "Something is missing," would go away. It didn't.

It wasn't until I actually had it all that I realized the whole thing was an illusion. The veil covering my eyes was lifted, spurred by the death of my dad. I understood whether you're in a fancy cage or a dilapidated one, it does not matter—a cage is still a cage. The security the cage provides is yet another illusion. It's as false as the notion you have to work to earn money, allowing energy to support you instead.

When my dad died, I saw everything in my human life was temporary, and the rug could be pulled from underneath me at any time—not only by death, but also in my career and my marriage. Nothing was a given anymore. All of it, all of the life I had built, could change with one phone call.

And once you see the truth—that everything is constantly shifting, security is an illusion, and nothing is really "safe" for the human—once you stare it in the face, there is no unseeing it. There is no pretending. You can pop some antidepressant or antianxiety pills to make the bars of the cage less visible. You can drink wine to numb the knowing that you are only half living, but it is always there—the familiar dull ache that won't go away.

I know because I tried it all. Shortly after my dad died, I went to see a doctor for my own sleeping pill prescription. The doctor handed me a questionnaire about depression and anxiety. I was honest but also let him know my dad recently died, and it was, of course, traumatic. I explained it was totally normal for me to experience grief and anxiety in this situation. I told him I was seeing a therapist weekly. He filled a sleeping pill prescription and wrote me another for an SSRI, a selective serotonin reuptake inhibitor, which is a class of drugs used to treat depression and anxiety.

He didn't tell me anything about the drug, and I honestly cannot remember the name of it—only that it smelled rancid, of chemicals and sulfur, and made me extremely ill and disoriented. I was such a wreck and so confused I tried the drug—completely ignoring my gut instinct it wasn't necessary and would, in fact, negatively impact my ability to hear my soul or master voice within.

My therapist recommended I stay in the marriage for at least a year after my dad died; she didn't want me to make any rash decisions. Well, I reasoned, if I listened to that soul voice, I would walk out of this marriage today, at that very moment.

If I popped these pills, maybe I could make it through the year, following my therapist's advice.

"Maybe I am the crazy one after all," I thought.

This was not my first SSRI rodeo. My mom stuffed Prozac down my throat when my father became ill for the first time when I was sixteen years old. She was on it too. It made me feel unlike myself, and my behavior changed quickly. I felt like a robot.

Suddenly, all those unwritten rules society placed on me seemed reasonable. Suddenly, it was me who was the problem rather than mass consciousness. I was the insane one, the world outside me the rational one. Maybe they were right. I was so messed up in the stories I was told about myself, the soul voice I had trusted so much was now labeled a voice in my head—one that needed to be ignored or, worse, eradicated.

At sixteen, it had never occurred to me, because my mom and my doctor had been so sure, it was quite normal to feel sad and anxious while my dad was in a hospital for eight long months.

Now, at thirty-two, after the childhood memories came back into my consciousness, I knew a sad situation warranted sad human emotions. Maybe it was no so bad to allow myself the time to feel them. What if instead of pumping myself full of drugs, I could return to the I Exist, the inner knowing human situations were but tiny drops in the bucket of the vast experience of the soul?

What if I could see from an expanded point of view, my dad's health issues and his death were part of his soul's journey and mine as well? What if I could honor it instead and allow myself to grieve uninhibited by a tiny soul-destroying pill?

After a week, the disgusting, filthy, chemical, stinking SSRIs went into the trash can where they belonged. As I threw them away, I realized those little pills were the modern version of mental institutions, where you didn't even know you were being locked up—institutions with invisible bars. I realized society wasn't any freer than it had been, say, twenty years ago; society was simply much more sophisticated at hiding the bars on the cages in the zoo.

I wish I had done the same at sixteen, tossing the Prozac into the trash can where it belonged, but it had drowned out the soul voice almost immediately as I began taking it. Also, I don't think it was any coincidence my drug addiction kicked in shortly after I began taking the Prozac daily.

The authority figures around me told me both with their words and behaviors, if you experienced so-called negative emotions you were supposed to numb them immediately, to push them aside as quickly as possible instead of feeling them and allowing them to flow.

To me, it didn't matter if the drug was legal or not. The law is and never was mine. My father taught me that; he knew when to bend the rules and when to break them. And let me tell you, cocaine makes you feel a hell of a lot better than Prozac. Prozac numbed me to a point where I felt I was barely living. Cocaine made me feel full of life, even if it was a total illusion. In hindsight, I was trying to balance out the numb feeling, the dull ache, with something that made me feel alive.

I could have found my solace in nature, in the magic of the trees and in connection with other realms and beings like I had as a child, but those worlds were shut off with the swallowing of the pill my mom handed to me each morning. That green-and-white pill seemed to pull a veil over my eyes through which I could only view the physical reality, and it blocked out all the others I discovered as a young girl.

My husband supported the doctor. He read articles online and diagnosed me as bipolar. In his defense, a soul awakening can look a hell of a lot like the symptoms for bipolar disorder, especially to someone living a singular human experience. He wanted to control me; he had been for years. He told me I was too sensitive, repeatedly, words I had heard all my

70

life, discrediting me at the soul level and my unique abilities and experiences.

This time he was too late to the game; my soul had already seeped in through the cracks the grief had so artfully created during my dad's coma. It probably happened while he was on one of his business trips. The inner knowing, or *gnost*, was undeniable: I was not insane, not too sensitive. My soul voice was there inside of me, and I was going to let it roar like a lion. And that's why I had to leave. One person living the illusion cannot coexist with another who knows it's all fake. And they certainly cannot have children together.

In mass consciousness, what my then husband offered was appealing. He had a nice cage in the zoo. I knew he would immediately find a woman to replace me. He did quickly; she was lovely, and I was happy for him. Truly. Although easier to leave than my marriage, my job was the same. I experienced the realization I was leaving one well-decorated cage each morning only to arrive at the other well-decorated cage where I worked. The pattern of work, wife, and workout felt like the movie *Groundhog Day*.

The foundation I worked for boasted stellar benefits, bonuses, unlimited vacation, a gym, showers, and free yoga classes. If you were going to work, this was a great place to do it. If I was going to have a white-picket-fence life, my then husband was the one to do it with. It wasn't the foundation or him I despised so much; it was the institution of 'should' and 'supposed to.' It was the bars on the cage I could not un-see. I could not go back into playing a role once I saw it was a role and not reality.

The limited menu of human experience became even more pronounced when I quit my job. I was asked the following: Was I pregnant? Had another organization swiped me away? How much did they offer? They could beat it. Was my husband being transferred? Did I need to take a sabbatical?

Once I realized it for myself, it became so obvious to me everyone around me was living in a cage at the zoo too. These were wonderfully decorated and adorned cages, but still cages nonetheless. The illusion of freedom was so artfully designed that people did not even know they were in one. They even pitied and raised money for the so-called oppressed in situations where the bars on the cage were more pronounced.

After I noticed the cage I lived in—that everyone around me seemed so happy to live in—I was floored. I was as angry as I had been at eight years old when I felt I was so different from my peers. I couldn't understand why no one else could see what I was seeing. I felt insane, yet I knew I was not. I wanted so desperately to show them. Like anyone else who becomes aware, the desire to educate felt heavy.

Please excuse my barrage of enlightened, anti-status quo Facebook memes while I blow up your feed.

I went through what almost everyone goes through when they awaken to something new. I believed it was my job to educate everyone around me, the human twisting the story of the soul into oblivion. In an energetic conversation with my soul, I realized the people around me did not want to see what I was seeing. Before my dad died, I would not have wanted to see it either. I was perfectly happy living in the illusion, under the hypnosis.

It seemed easier and more comfortable to have your life laid out in front of you in a ten-to-twenty-year plan in which you choose between the chicken, beef, fish, or vegetarian item on the menu. Not knowing what was next was unpleasant to the human.

It could only be tolerated, or even embraced, in a state of awareness only found when in alignment with the soul. The soul journey wasn't for everyone. Had I not experienced many human lives living in the illusion before getting to this point? Was that not a valuable experience? Could I simply honor and respect the choices of others instead?

In this conversation, I realized true compassion is honoring everyone and every situation around you—and here's the kicker—without trying to change them or it. The desire to educate or enlighten those around me was coming from the human part of myself rather than from the I Exist. The soul never needs to force the people around it to change using illusory power. Simply living my life awake was radical enough, and I did not need to shove my realizations down other people's throats.

As quickly as the realization had occurred, my human self forgot it. There was that amnesia again, the one experienced repeatedly in the density of the physical body. I continued to try to explain what I was going through to others, realizing the illusion of freedom was very convincing.

When I did try to discuss it with others, their brains would be sent into instant overload—if they could handle listening to me for more than a minute. If they did take the time to hear me out, their eyes glazed over as they quickly labeled me as either a grieving person who would soon recover or as mentally unstable before excusing themselves as quickly as possible. I'll admit it, I didn't make much sense at the time. Everything was muddled in the constant and incessant negotiation and mediation between the voices of the human and the soul.

As in India, my soul voice came in clearly, and then it would go through the filter of the human mind, which would distort the wisdom beyond recognition. After repeating this pattern several hundred thousand times, I finally realized I needed to reroute the soul communication away from the human filters of thought and emotion and declare the soul voice the sole voice. No more negotiating with antiquated human logic. It would take years of experience.

In a last-ditch effort to stay in my marriage, my human self proposed he quit his job too and we live in a van, travel around, and surf. Maybe we should try 'freedom' for a change. Maybe we should put off having a baby for a little while longer. He looked at me like I had lost my mind, his bipolar wife making an insane suggestion. Yet, I realized there was no putting it off. For me, having a child with anyone felt like an eighteen-year prison sentence.

About a year into our marriage, I found myself driving past a youth club, where I saw the line of cars full of exhausted moms waiting to pick their kids up from their sporting activities. In that moment my stomach churned, and I began to sweat with anxiety. It was not what I wanted for my life. I saw my friends having kids with so much love for the experience, but no matter how hard I tried to change my feelings, I knew it wasn't for me.

After we split up, I realized my husband was not wrong or bad demanding I produce a child. I was not a bad person for not wanting one. We both behaved in ways others would find offensive. While the fight was ongoing, my human self was keeping score. One blow by him was met with another blow from me. Once I moved out of the house and could see it with fresh eyes, I realized the concepts of good and bad, right and wrong, and positive and negative were all human creations.

When I moved beyond the dualistic constructs, I saw everything—and I truly mean everything—is good and bad, and neither good nor bad. It was the human brain that wanted to label it one or the other. My then husband did his best to love me and support me, *and* he was an asshole. I was going through a massive transformation, *and* I had broken the promises I had made to him, all while acting totally insane. Nothing is as black and white as the human tries to make it.

The more I connected with my soul, the more I could see the *and* in everything. I saw and sensed my soul didn't operate in or really even comprehend dualities. It operated in experiences and expressions without labeling them as positive or negative. It took a while longer for my human self to get it. My brain desperately wanted to keep everything in nice, neat categories—to label others as the villain, to blame the doctor for my dad's death. Instead, Sar'h, in her deep, sensual voice, reminded me my marriage was an amazing experience and taught me many things, including how to love myself and listen to the soul voice.

Instead of blaming someone for my dad's death, my soul took an expanded perspective. My dad parted with this world at the perfect moment. His death spurred an awakening inside me before I brought a child into this world. His death allowed me the freedom to do what I had set out to do at the soul level, and he had left me some pocket change to get me going. His death was a gift that afforded me the time and space to breathe into the awareness of the soul and what a relationship with it had to offer me—true freedom. No menus, no cages, no pills.

And beyond, later I realized it was all just an act—one that doesn't need to be analyzed. Yet, I really feel like I needed to put the prison I found myself stuck at the time into this book, so you could see where it leads, and what it looks like to move beyond the play of human life.

I had no idea what my life would look like outside of the cage. I didn't even know what I was going to order; I only knew it would be off the menu. Freedom is scary as fuck. When people say they want freedom, what most actually mean is they want a little bit more—a little bit more money, a nicer car, more vacation days—a bigger, nicer cage in the zoo. Freedom is a different beast entirely. It's what exists beyond the walls of the zoo. Further, freedom only exists when you have released all the roles of human identity through multiple and seemingly endless deaths of Self.

It felt like completely uncharted territory at the time, and I didn't have much to go on, only the sense and the inner knowing I could not stay inside its walls. I finally busted through the bars inside of myself. I filed for divorce in June 2013. The human part of me felt lost, barely keeping her head above water in the chaos of consciousness. Inside me, fireworks were going off in celebration of the soul's return. I was two people at once, and it felt completely natural. I felt more myself than I had in years. I was the four-year-old under the kitchen table again. I Exist, nothing else really mattered, yet fresh out of the zoo, I needed somewhere to live.

8 THE SUNNY SHACK

SUMMER 2013

After I began divorce proceedings, I needed to find a place to live, and nothing seemed to be working out. It took a good, long while for my human self to realize the soul doesn't worry about human things like where you are going to live, and sometimes you have to tell it, "Hey, dude, I know you're doing your thing and all, but this human expression needs a place to call home. If we're going to do this thing, I need to be comfortable."

In my new state of awareness post awakening, I was not praying to God, begging the universe for signs or answers, getting angry with God or the universe, practicing the law of attraction or creating a vision board for fuck's sake. I was searching inside myself for a creative solution—a soul solution.

Simultaneously, my human self desperately tried to come up with a plan. My soon to be ex-husband was out of the country, and I had four weeks to vacate what had once been our home. I had not yet come to a place where I trusted my inner voice in the complete way I eventually would. Further, in the realized state once the soul and human selves combined, these things just seem to take care of themselves without even a thought or care. But here is where I was at the time.

"Ha! You want a plan?" I imagined my soul lightheartedly laughing. "There is no plan. Only creation."

Eventually—I am a slow learner—I stopped wasting energy on plans. Letting go of plans, goals, budgets, and expectations for myself was one of the hardest parts of moving from my human aspect controlling my life to living a soul-driven life. And it did not happen overnight. It was a long process with many steps forward—only to fall back down to the bottom of the stairs sometimes.

As a conscious creator—one who is aware of the true creative nature of the soul—goals, plans, and linear time become completely obsolete—something I had known so intensely as a child, for example, when I brought Mortimer into my physical world. I knew how energy worked and responded to consciousness back then, but there were a few decades if not lifetimes of programming to defragment.

I later remembered when the soul creates, it is not to meet the definition of success that comes from an external source. The soul knows no external force. Instead, the soul creates to express itself, simply for the joy of creation. It creates for the experience rather than the outcome. It's totally different from how our parents, teachers, and coworkers showed us, where metrics are the norm. To authentically create, we must throw out the metrics.

I learned—the hard way as usual—the reason it is so imperative to let go of goals, plans, and the fear of so-called failure is because so often our soul's creative solutions are beyond the imagination of the human. Our human selves cannot even fathom the possibilities and potentials. So, when the human sets its eye on the prize, the goal, it narrows our vision so much, we cannot see the much grander possibilities and potentials our soul is presenting all around us to choose off the menu once again.

Unaware, my human self drove around desperately from apartment to apartment, and nothing seemed to be working out. The last apartment I looked at that day denied my application because of the drug charge on my record from 1999. Embarrassed, I went back to my car, Ollie sitting in the passenger's seat. I was hysterically crying when the phone rang. It was the realtor my soon-to-be ex and I had worked with before. I wiped my tears away and answered the call.

"Are you still interested in an investment property?"

"No, I can't do that right now," was my human thought. It was a plan I had made with my husband when I had a job—to invest in something besides the stock market—and I no longer had a husband or a job. Then I heard a deep voice from within. It was not words. It was not a feeling or emotion. It was a deep, sensual, inner knowing this was my creative solution.

"Yes, I am." I tried to sound sure, but I wasn't. I wiped the tears from my face.

He explained the owners of the house wanted to sell it quickly for a low price because it needed work. What did I know about fixing an old, dilapidated house? What if it was in total disrepair and I lost money? I could be out tens of thousands of dollars. Yet the soul voice told me in its' calm whisper, "Go take a look and see."

I took a few deep breaths, had a laugh at the soap opera, and I typed the address into my phone and drove to the house. The tenants still occupied the house, so my realtor and I could not go in. He climbed under the pier-and-beam foundation to check it out anyway.

"I think we can make some money off this house," he said.

My real estate agent was a father figure to me, and I trusted him. I looked at the house. It was a fucking mess, even from the outside. A broken chain link fence rimmed the backyard. When I peered through the window, I saw a washing machine from the 1980s sat in the kitchen, which looked like no one had cleaned it since they put the washer in.

"Where do you put the clothes dryer?" I asked my agent. He opened the garage door, which was covered in termite holes, and pointed at the dryer inside. A family of cockroaches ran across the floor. And yet my soul said, "This is it. Buy it." With his help, I made the offer. I went to the bank for the loan; it was approved instantly.

The situation reminded me of a woman I once knew. She had no credit, two children, and needed to get away from an alcoholic husband. A bank loan was one of her last options. She told me she met with a banker who said there was no way she could get the loan.

Then something changed in the banker's eyes—like someone hit the reset button on his brain. He shuffled through her paperwork once more and then asked to be excused for a minute.

He came back with a loan check for ten thousand dollars—exactly what she needed to make a new start. She knew enough to know when what you want shows up on your doorstep, you don't wait around for people to realize what's going on or that they made a mistake; you take your check and get the hell out of there.

I had the keys to the house in one week. Everything seemed so easy. That's when I was able to convince my human self this was not crazy. When things flow, when things fall into place with such ease and grace, that's where the magic happens.

When things get plugged up, it's time to step back and reroute. My agent, his wife, and I somehow coordinated a plumber, handyman, tile guy, and electrician. There were a few hiccups, like opening the refrigerator and discovering it was completely covered in black mold spores, and a few triumphs, like fitting a brand-new stackable washer and dryer in place of the water heater so it wouldn't be split in the kitchen and garage.

I also had to kick out the tenant, who had been given a year's notice yet still had the personality of the Unabomber. Regardless, we had the house up and running in six weeks, and I wasn't too bothered I spent five thousand dollars more on the renovations than budgeted because the price of the house was so low.

We painted the shutters and the doors outside the seven-hundred-square-foot yellow house a vibrant orange. With no family to help me move, my girlfriends stepped in.

When Teresa came over to unpack my belongings and decorate, she dubbed it the Sunny Shack. It was the perfect name. Little did I know the Sunny Shack would serve as my home base as I traveled all over the world for the next two years, my new reality exceeding any human expectation I'd ever had for my life.

When I hit the two-year mark of owning the house—to avoid taxes you must occupy a home for two years before selling it—I called my agent and said I might be ready to sell it. No problem, he said. Within one week, he sold that old shack in June 2015 for a mighty profit, funding my adventures for yet another year. It was totally above and beyond anything my human self could have planned for—the same person who could not rent an apartment because they were addicted to drugs in 1999, the same one hysterically crying in the car. The *and* of the Self.

Had I operated solely as my human expression—ordering off the menu handed to me—I would have taken another job to simply pay rent and make ends meet as I worked a full-time desk job and looked for the next husband all my friends kept saying was on the way any day now.

Instead, I listened to my inner voice. To the human self, it looked like a big risk; to the soul, it was the creative solution I had asked for. I funded my adventures without compromising my true soul's desire to allow in ease instead of work toward some strange external goal.

Sure, people thought I was nuts, including my human self, but screw them and their advice. When you're in the flow, the last thing you need is to listen to human, fear-based advice from your mind or the minds of people around you.

Later, when my human expression screamed we need a plan for a storm that might or might not come, my soul flashed the image of the Sunny Shack. Its canary-yellow walls and sunset-orange shutters reminded me once again the grandest creations come from the soul and the fountain of creativity that flows from within.

It reminded me I could tap into the fountain of ever-abundant energy within, rather than grasping for energy outside myself like the majority of humanity that yelled, "More. More. More." More flowed from with me; it was not something I grabbed at from the external.

Somewhere in between leaving my marriage and moving into the Sunny Shack in June 2013, I was out with my former college roommate. We had just arrived at a music venue and stood outside, beers in hand, when I heard someone yell my name.

I couldn't tell where it came from. Then he emerged from the crowd. It was Mr. C, one of the long-haired boys with guitars who had been in my junior high crew. I was over the moon to see him. About sixteen years had passed since I'd last seen him.

"No fucking way!"

We hugged, caught up, and reminisced. I'd probably smoked my first joint with him and his best friend, Kevin, but I'd lost touch when I started hanging out with the cool kids.

Seeing him instantly opened some sort of door for me, and all the memories came flooding back in—not only of our days attending concerts and smoking cigarettes in the bushes of suburbia, but all my esoteric studies.

His presence alone was enough to take me back to the place of my eleven-to-fifteen-year-old self, who was so in touch with her soul voice, who knew exactly who she was and was not.

I desperately wanted to reclaim her. I also wondered where along the path to success I'd lost my love of music and the effects it had on me at both the soul and human levels. It was time to bring both the music and the magic back in.

I ended up seeing Mr. C many times throughout the summer of 2013 before he moved away. In a strange twist in my newly single life in the Sunny Shack, I made a friend who was also single. Liz had recently met and begun dating a guy named John, who lived in another city but came to his lake home on the weekends.

I went out to the lake house with them one weekend only to find Mr. C and his best friend hanging out too. It was all too designed to be a coincidence. The strange crew we formed spent the summer playing in the lake like teenagers with bigger budgets. We would swim, blast the radio on the boat, and dance away the day in our bathing suits, cocktails in hand, watching the sun set every Friday and Saturday night. I felt like a teenager again, totally free from responsibility and the unwritten rules placed on adults.

It was a summer of love, wine, dancing, sunsets on the lake, motorcycle rides, and rock and roll, and I was having a great time. I felt younger than I had in years. The weight of a career, marriage, and being my father's caregiver melted off me. When I looked in the mirror, I appeared younger and more beautiful than ever. I was falling in love with the freedom of this new life, and most importantly, I was falling in love with myself for the first time.

As the end of summer grew near, I felt the pull from my soul to return to the path I had veered from in my adolescence. With the final release of the human responsibilities I had so fiercely hung onto for so long, the path didn't feel so far away this time. I understood on some level all this fun was about allowing my human expression of Self to be fully human, to have the maximum experience of what it had to offer. There was no family, husband, or job standing in the way—no rules I was trying to live by.

The summer ended on cue. There were no more weekends of

debauchery at the lake on the weekends as John packed up and headed to home to be with his children. Liz and I wrapped up the summer nicely with a weekend at a music festival.

That Saturday after the last band played, we got on our bikes to ride home. A quick rain shower made the roads slick. Flying down the street, my front bike wheel slid, and I came crashing down, hitting my bare head on the concrete so hard I could feel it bounce.

I lay in my front bedroom of the Sunny Shack for three days after the music festival, unable to move much—my entire body aching from the accident. As I mentioned before, so often accidents are an opportunity for more of our soul to seep back into our physical bodies.

Bump and fill. I had not thought much about the incident at the time. A somewhat drunk girl in a bike accident after a music festival was not abnormal. However, my behavior after the incident tells another story.

The Texas version of fall was approaching. In the winds of the changing season, I felt the internal pull to shift directions. Suddenly, I had no interest in bass playing, Harley-riding lovers, or weekends of debauchery. Intuitively, I turned inward, and by October and November it would manifest in such a way, there was no way to deny who I was or what I was here to experience.

9 THE SERPENT YEARS

AUGUST 2011—NOVEMBER 2013
WEST TEXAS & SACRED VALLEY, PERU

My human expression tended to think everything in life was happening in linear time—like the human was a little black dot moving along a timeline in a history book.

However, I began to experience life from the body of wisdom that is the soul—or the mastery that is the sum of all wisdom distilled from every lifetime and in between. In this reality, I became the fixed point of consciousness through which time and space moved.

One way I heard it described later—simply to lend a somewhat confusing topic additional language—was time and space move through me—the single point of consciousness—rather than me moving through time and space.

I experienced moments of this energetic phenomena come and go and later in my self-realized state it would become a permanent fixture of my reality.

However, if I need to I can view the linear perspective in order to communicate with those around me. Pulling myself small to get physical things done, for example, and then allowing the return to the natural state being beyond linearity to return with ease.

That being said, for the purpose of this book, I aimed to write my experiences in layers, keeping some sort of linear timeline. Often too much occurred at any given moment to put into one chapter designated for the point in time.

This chapter goes back to the time when my father was in a coma, his death, and my marriage falling apart to describe what was going on in my soul evolution, rather than being focused on my physical human reality as I did in the previous chapters.

My consciousness began to expand inexplicably and uncoaxed when I sat next to my comatose father as he hung onto life by a thin thread. His soul hung outside his body as he made the decision whether to live or die, and it thinned the veil between the physical and nonphysical realms so much, I found I existed in both again simultaneously, like I had as a child.

It was then the life force energy some call kundalini—others simply call it Spirit (individualized)—began to stir in the base of my spine and fill my womb with a pulsing electric energy.

It felt as if someone had hooked an electric cord into my uterus and the base of my spine and turned up the voltage to high. What a strange scene to think about now. Me, sitting in the most unsacred of places, holding the swollen, freezing-cold hand of a near-dead man who was hooked up to every machine possible, having a metaphysical experience.

At the time, I had no idea what it meant or what the feeling was, and I was too exhausted from trying to take care of my father, be somewhat of a good employee, and fulfill the bare minimum of my wifely duties to figure out what was happening to me. The intense electric pulse would come and go over the coming months and years as I watched my human life unravel.

In retrospect, it's easy to see the then-unknown force was driving my decisions, which seemed entirely insane and reckless to the outside world and the human voice inside of me, which was almost completely unaware of what was going on. I only knew what I could not do. The longer I stayed in situations not in alignment with my soul, the sicker I got. It made me ill to go to work. The last four months of my marriage, I was swollen, lethargic, and appeared to be allergic to everything I put into my mouth. I saw doctor after doctor, and none could say what was wrong with me. I avoided gluten and then meat. I drank only juice, and nothing seemed to work.

Eventually, when I moved into the Sunny Shack, my health dramatically improved without medical care or the box of supplements I took during the last months of the marriage. I could eat again without it swelling me into oblivion.

The nearly twenty pounds I could not lose no matter what I tried suddenly fell off my small frame. The daily patterns of my marriage and my job had been making me ill—this energy activating inside of me seemed to act as a repellant to things not in alignment with my awakening, of which I was in complete denial about at the human level of awareness.

As I began to clean up the rubble of my wrecked life, snakes—or the proverbial serpent—began to impose physically upon my life. On a walk with my dog in October 2012, right after I told my husband for the first time I did not think I could be married anymore, I came across a thick, solid-black snake coiled tightly on the sidewalk.

I lived along a creek for six years and never seen anything like it. I might have shrugged it off as a coincidence, but snakes continued to appear in record numbers.

A week later a snake slithered through my fingers while I was gardening. The next day a snake fell out of a tree and wrapped itself around my husband's arm. A silver snake crossed my path on a trail, and then a water moccasin swam across the surface of the lake where my dog had paddled through—all within the same week.

By April 2013, my husband was so used to my snake attraction, he did not even bat an eyelash when a six-foot rat snake came into my mother's house through a dog door on Easter Sunday. The following month—May 2013, one year after my father's death—we both headed to Big Bend National Park with friends. Once again, a six-foot-long, black-and-white-striped snake slithered across our path. The last night of the trip I experienced a dream that would change everything.

Over the last eight months—or the year of the snakes as I somewhat jokingly called it—I dreamed of snakes nearly every night in addition to seeing them while awake. That final night in my West Texas dreams, I found myself in some sort of shamanic Native American ceremony. The drums rhythmically pounded while the people danced and sang. In the middle of their circle, a mythic, almost cartoon-like cobra began to uncoil. At the height of the drumming, the cobra reached its full height, and its hood reached full width. It stared directly into my eyes, stuck out its split tongue, and hissed with an indescribable intensity.

I woke up in a panic and a sweat. I knew undoubtedly it was time to leave the marriage. As much as my human did not want to, I knew the natural and undeniable soul evolution I was experiencing could not take place within its walls. I also knew deeply on some level the snake was an expression of me, of Self, and it was coaxing me with its dance to allow my awakening to uncoil not only inside my body but in my whole life. It was an invitation to accept my awakening as my new reality, and stop denying the inevitable as I had for so many years. And accept, I finally did.

By late summer and early fall 2013, I was living on my own in the Sunny Shack. We finalized the divorce. Freeing up the energies I'd needed to get to work and be a wife, I found I redirected them to my soul's evolution, naturally. My human expression continued to be pretty much blind as to what was occurring, yet that was about to change.

One person once told me I stayed asleep as long as I possibly could. They were right. Awakening is a tiny, short burst of bliss and then it becomes quite the beast. I'm glad mine didn't last too long before realization set in in the fall of 2017. If I thought the dark night of the soul was bad, it would be a cake walk compared to the complete annihilation of Self that delivered me on the door step of my own self-realization.

On October 11, 2013, I attended my regular Friday night yoga class, as I often did before going out drinking with my friends. I know before I said I released the collective yogi consciousness, and I had. Yet, I loved the way the practice made my body feel and how it helped balance my energy—I still do, and I move in its poses every single day. However, I quit kidding myself there was anything in the texts—ancient or modern—that was going to support this unfoldment of Self.

At the end of class, I sat in silent meditation with the others when I began to feel my spine move involuntarily, slithering and spinning clockwise. The electric current was no longer active only in the base of the spine and the uterus but was slowly, yet with increasing intensity, creeping up my spine.

Once it reached the base of the neck, I began to experience a high like no other—and I've done a lot of drugs in my life—yet felt completely sober, aware and observing.

With my eyes closed, I saw every color in the rainbow and colors I didn't have a name for. Time and space no longer existed. I was in a void, the place of no place, the space of no time.

My human self was aware enough to be thankful to be sitting in a dark room where people could not see my jarring movements. Even though my eyes were closed, I felt as if they were open, and I was seeing the world for the first time.

I felt my internal vision open to a 360-degree view, expanding like the hood of the cobra visiting me in the West Texas dream. I observed the experience both from inside my body and outside it.

This was not like observing my body from outside like after my father died. It was an expansion of Self. I expanded so much from the point of the I Exist, I could see in all directions. My soul was not detached from the body. Everything was in alignment—soul and human as one expression of the I Am.

The yoga instructor began talking again, something about controlling the fluctuations of the mind, which made me want to laugh out loud and flip him off at the same time, and just like that, the experience was over.

My body, led by my spine, spiraled counterclockwise as the electric current swirled back down into the base of the spine, exactly like that tightly coiled black snake first appearing to me one year before.

One month later—November 2013—I found myself in a beautiful retreat center in the Sacred Valley of Peru, where I was completing an advanced yoga teacher training. This time the training was not to find answers, but rather to enjoy the experience of new friends and lots of physical practice in a beautiful location.

On a break between sessions, I sat in a lush, green garden meditating when I heard some fellow students playing music—various drum and tambourine beats accompanied by guttural sounds of the women dancing and chanting wildly in a circle. I stood up from my meditation and went to sit in the middle of the dancing women, who were uninterrupted by my presence.

The electric current began to rise up the spine as my body moved rapidly in a clockwise motion. This time after my 'hood' expanded and I came into my magnified vision, the energy shot up through the crown of my head for the first time, rather than becoming stuck in my neck like in the yoga studio.

With it, my consciousness followed. I was in a snake's body, an expression of Self, as it jetted into the gardens. I was clearly seeing out of the eye slits of a snake. At the same time in my body, I felt an incontrollable urge to allow the spine to create a wavelike motion, mimicking the slither of a moving snake. Then I moved my awareness back to the snake I simultaneously embodied, slithering and writhing through the grass outside the room where the music was taking place.

Again, time and space were suspended as I traveled through the lush gardens in my snake body. It was as concrete as I describe, and the only thing I have to compare it to is a psychedelic-drug experience, which I will add is completely subpar to this completely natural one.

After what seemed like hours but was really probably about five to ten minutes, I came back into my slithering human body and felt the electric current slowly recoil back down into the base of the spine.

Later, I learned the experience was what some call a kundalini awakening—I had never heard the term before, and it was not covered in my yoga teacher trainings. *Kundalini* is a Sanskrit word meaning "coiled one" and is often represented as a sleeping serpent that lies at the base of the spine, waiting to be awakened.

In yogic theories, when kundalini or primal earth-force energy awakens, it moves up central channels along the spine to the crown of the head through energy centers called chakras. A kundalini awakening is often considered part of the spiritual enlightenment experience in many cultures.

While this is a gross oversimplification of kundalini in the context of yogic theory, I must state while it is one way to describe my effortless and unplanned by the human experience, my views vary widely from those of the yogic community, some of whom try to activate this energy, when to me it is about allowing it to awaken.

For me, I see it as this—the date of your awakening is set long before you come into physical form. It either happens naturally or it doesn't and will in the next few lifetimes. Trying to make it happen before you are ready is fruitless, and on occasion, it is dangerous.

Today, I understand the experience as simply an infusion of consciousness, or pure awareness with energy responding to that consciousness—a massive integration of my soul, my spirit into the physical body. Really, the label on the experience didn't matter; the effect it had on my reality did. I was fully awake, and I had no idea what to do with it.

10 MORTIMER, MERLIN, AND MASTER MORYA

OCTOBER 2013

Running parallel to this infusion of serpent energy, I became aware of the name of the tall, thin Indian friend who had been with me in on the vibrating island, and when I sensed into it, I felt his presence in India had not been the first.

Before I can take you forward, I have to take you back to October 8, 2013. It was three days prior to the energy releasing in the base of my spine in the dark yoga class, and it was certainly no coincidence.

Knowing I was devastated after my father's death and the collapse of my marriage, a longtime girlfriend of mine, Alison, recommended I speak with a medium. She was the family friend of Alison's good friend. She had the gift of being able to talk to those who had crossed over or left the physical body. In other words, she saw and spoke with dead people. It took me months to get on her busy schedule, and finally the day arrived. We held the meeting on Skype. I'll admit I was skeptical of this woman and careful not to give her too much background information as a test to see if she was really, in fact, able to communicate with my father.

I visited with my dad in a dream in January, eight months prior, after pleading with him for help on one of the worst days in my marriage. Afterward, I felt his presence intensely. A few times I saw a white orb hovering around me, but I felt blocked in being able to communicate with him. My human brain still had muscle and continued to place doubt in the ability to see, feel, and know beyond the five basic human senses.

The medium started out our Skype session by welcoming 'my angels' to appear. Immediately, she informed me my father was present, as was my great-grandmother, Helen, whom I never physically met in this life but who had been close to my mother as a child. She was the mother of my maternal grandfather, Spud.

Finally, there was a third being who introduced himself as El Morya. When the medium said his name, I felt a tingle shoot up my spine. In my inner vision, I saw a man with a thin face, dark beard, and large brown eyes. His energy felt entirely different from my dad's and Helen's, who were chatting with me in the near-Earth realms. They felt human; he felt wise, expanded. My intuition allowed me to trust him instantly, and I was excited with what he had to share with me.

My father had much to say as usual. He cleared up some details around his death, such as why his wife acted the way she had in the weeks after his memorial service. Dealing with her and her family had been a total nightmare. My dad indicated outside forces out of her control strongly influenced her behavior, something I understood all too well. I allowed forgiveness of myself for reacting so poorly and called her in the next few days to say 'hey, I honor you and what you did for my dad in his last years of life.' I didn't do it for her. I did for myself, so I could move on. Finally.

My dad sounded so much like himself, and the medium indicated, as she translated his words, he talked with his hands in broad gestures. My doubts about her ability to communicate with him completely faded away. Additionally, I felt his unconditional love wash over me like it had in his physical presence. It was a specific sensation, like his love for me had its own frequency on the radio dial, and I knew it was him.

The medium explained to me my dad had one foot in this world and one in the spirit world, and he was laying stones for me. He would be traveling with me to Peru, where I was headed in November.

Also, for the past month, a blue jay had been ever present on my daily walks and in my backyard. I did not bring this up to the medium, but in the reading my father communicated to me this represented him visiting me. This knowledge brought indescribable comfort to me at the time. I had felt so lost without him, only to learn he was there with me the whole time; he simply lacked a human body.

Helen had an earful about my love life and was very displeased on how my soon-to-be ex-husband had been treating me. She explained it was a karmic relationship and said I would find love again.

In this moment, I was simply overjoyed to hear my dad was well and enjoying his experiences on the other side. He told me he and his father, Cecil, went sailing—it was confirmation of the January dream where he bobbed in the ocean, beaming his giant, trademark smile at me back on shore.

My dad and Helen also had a mouthful about my near future. They told me through the medium I would meet the love of my life within the next year and have two kids. My human expression loved to hear this, and my soul sighed heavily.

"Here we go again," my soul said in sensations. "These kind of prophecies and psychic predictions of fairy tale human lives are the biggest distractions of all from the Return to Self."

Later that day, Sar'h explained to me people in the near-earth realms didn't know any more about the future than me because it wasn't written in stone. As sovereign, self-governing beings, we choose what our lives will look like.

On some level, I was angry with them for sharing this. Dead people are not any more psychic because they are dead; many a person has based their life trajectory on such things. My father and Helen saw no more clearly than me. If they were, in fact, psychic, the only thing psychics have the ability to see is future potentials and possibilities, often through a limited lens.

At the time, the aspect of myself that believed in the Prince Charming fairy tale still had an active voice within me, and it was annoying as hell. For the next year, the damsel-in-distress aspect would desperately look for her prince everywhere we went because my dad, an authority figure, had declared it so.

Let's just say he never came; my dad was wrong. This was the beginning of my understanding that in addition to the soul and human voices, there were also the voices of many aspects coming into play.

Today I see "aspects" as identities our souls created in the past to answer the question, "Who am I?" They serve a role in our current or previous lives, and the natural progression is for the identity to integrate once it is no longer serving a role. Instead, these rogue identities often take on their own voices and cause chaos and confusion in our lives if we are not conscious, or aware of them.

Sometimes we create aspects to fill roles in certain situations, like daughter, wife, or business owner. Additionally, past-life identities come into play, even ones created in dreams and other realities. I once dealt with an aspect in my bedroom whose face morphed into another, changing every second. That was interesting.

When we are unconscious of them, the rogue identities can drag us in all directions. They can literally haunt us. On most occasions, when I thought I was dealing with a ghost or Earth-bound spirit, it turned out to be an old, unintegrated aspect haunting me.

It would take me another year and a half to figure out what these rogue voices were and, most importantly, instead of running them off by burning sage and wrapping myself in white light, and all the other New Age tricks and hoopla, I actually needed to invite them into the soul for integration.

It's really as easy as this—once we become aware of the old roles and rogue identities they integrated themselves on their own—without any effort on behalf of the human expression of Self. I just needed to take a deep breath and gather some human patience.

This being named El Morya remained silent and patient as my dad and Helen went back and forth about the human details of my life. I could sense he was going to share some wisdom when it came to the path of the soul, which was what I was really interested in, what really made my heart beat.

"El Morya"—the name seemed so foreign to me as I jotted it down in my notebook, not knowing how it was spelled. Yet when he spoke, I knew it was time to listen carefully, and there would be no garble about my human love life.

First, he told me I had a very awakened third eye, which was the language I could understand at the time. What he was saying was I was conscious; I could see beyond the physical. He meant I was wiser than I could remember or fathom at the time.

"No shit, Sherlock," I thought.

I already knew this, but then I realized there was more to his words. Suddenly, it brought up a memory from December, when I'd returned from India. I was Christmas shopping for the last holiday with my husband's family.

I was in Barney's when I saw a tiny gold necklace with a third eye hanging from it, a tiny diamond forming the pupil of the eye. It called to me, and I asked the sales clerk to pull it from the case so I could try it on. I loved it. The price tag seemed a bit steep for something so trivial when I needed to be spending money on gifts.

"Consider it a gift from me, a reminder of who you are. A conscious being having a human experience. Remember what you came for."

The words delivered through sensations had come from my tall, thin Indian friend who had sat next to me on my yoga mat the previous month. In that moment, I finally connected the dots through the unrelenting density of the human mind.

"Holy hell!" The bells went off inside of me. "Ding. Ding. Ding!"

El Morya was the friend, the merlin, possibly even the Mortimer, who had been with me all these years. Now he was talking to me through a medium on a computer. It was an experience beyond my wildest human imagination. You couldn't make this shit up. It was undeniably true; this was happening.

As a child, it had seemed so natural to have these experiences, but the world around me pounded the magic of my childhood experiences into oblivion. I could feel the magic of life returning, and it was going to have nothing to do with Prince Charming and the two rug rats my dad and Helen spoke of.

Second, El Morya told me people would be drawn to me, and I should not be scared. He repeated it: "People will come to you, and you should not be scared."

"Okay," I thought. I couldn't fathom what he meant at the time, so I wrote it down to examine later. What people? Yet I wouldn't have to wait too long for the answer. A slew of disembodied professors, like Mortimer and El Morya, were already gathering in my living room.

Next, El Morya said, "You are very wise and on Earth to teach."

Another mentor of mine also told me repeatedly I would teach, but this information puzzled me as much as it did when Mortimer told me so many years ago I stored codes of truth within me.

What in the ever-living fuck did they all want me to teach? What did I have to share? I didn't feel equipped to teach anyone anything. I'd spent the summer making love, drinking wine, listening to music, and dancing on a boat deck. What did I know? Who would be coming to me for answers?

Yet his words passed my gut check, which was the end all be all for me at the time. I trusted him and the fact that the details were going to fill themselves in as usual.

The final thing El Morya told me was he knew I liked to be active, but I needed to be still and listen; what he meant was listen to the song of your soul. Pause and wait for the symphony of Self to echo through your own being-ness.

"I'm supposed to sit still." I shuddered. "Not my best talent."

My human expression wailed like a toddler throwing a tantrum and then quickly surrendered. The human ego part of me began to realize some fights with the will of the soul to know itself weren't worth it. When my hour was up, I thanked everyone before signing off Skype, thinking to myself how strange it all was.

Now I really wanted to know who El Morya was and how he knew so much about me, but the medium had simply shrugged her shoulders when asked. After our session was over, I did what anyone would do and hit up Google.

Now equipped with the Indian's name, I typed it in various configurations. Then it popped up. He was an ascended master. Deep internal pause. An ascended master. What is that?

My human expression never heard the term before. It took me some tries to figure out an ascended master was someone who had completed their cycle of lifetimes on Earth, becoming self-realized or enlightened like Buddha or Jesus.

"Or King Arthur, my childhood hero," I thought.

I learned there were many others like him, some better known than others. Today I understand roughly ten thousand human beings who have made their way through the enlightenment/ascension/self-realization experience, whatever you wish to call it.

Now, I sense, and I could be totally off, somewhere around three thousand beings on Earth in physical form, either stepping into mastery or are masters returning to Earth at this significant time. To clarify, I sense about one million finding themselves in the state of awakening and around several thousand are allowing their realization to unfold as I feel into this specific moment.

Sounds small — yes; however, I have a sense this is a record number of people in physical form having this experience. Today I personally know about ten of these people in a physical way. The rest I simply connect to in the ethers.

Through my research, I learned El Morya received his name in his last human incarnation as El Morya Kahn, who lived in India and ascended in 1898. The website listed his other incarnations on Earth included Abraham; Melchior, one of the three wise men at the birth of Jesus; and King Arthur—wait, what? King Arthur?

My mind was about to explode, unable to handle the infusion of energy shooting through my body. Later I would learn El Morya was also the teacher of Helena Blavatsky, the Russian occultist, spirit medium, and author who cofounded the Theosophical Society in 1875.

After the reading with the medium and in the following days, I began to go through a series of experiences in remembering with El Morya and other ascended masters. As it turned out, I no longer needed the medium to translate.

Later, I realized she, in fact, had no clue who or what an ascended master was. Just like many times after, I got as much information as I could from the seer/ healer/ teacher as I could and then quickly felt myself jammed up against the wall of their own consciousness limitations.

Later I learned El Morya was not a foreign teacher of sorts, rather he was an extremely old friend. Over the coming years, the understanding the lifetimes we held together unfurled — ones in Atlantis, one in which I played the role of his mother, another his wife. That's why he was able to show up in this medium reading. He was part of my soul's lineage. Wow.

My human self was floored. Was this what I had been doing as a child? It felt oddly familiar, and not just from childhood. I understood this was not a new ability. I had been doing this for thousands of years, eons. I all but forgot it in the density of the illusion the physical world created. My human voice finally admitted it did not seem so crazy I'd quit my job and left my marriage. There was so much more to life. I was reeling.

After the medium reading, many experiences rapidly unfolded. I received communications from beings not yet identified while I was driving, walking my dog, and often while sleeping in the middle of the night. My new friends led me on Internet searches at 3:00 a.m. I was happy to jump down Alice's rabbit hole, no matter how mad it made me.

During one of the 3:00 a.m. sessions, I landed on a website with an audio recording in which a woman was channeling El Morya while being interviewed by her husband in a radio-show format.

It felt as if El Morya spoke directly to me, and I realized the interview was recorded on October 6, 2013—two days before my reading with the medium. At the end of the interview, the husband of the channeler said, "If this recording called to anyone, they should contact us." Turns out they lived in the same area as me at the time. I had to call.

The next morning, I called the channeler. Her husband answered the phone and passed it over.

"How'd you hear about me?" she asked.

"El Morya sent me."

I felt ridiculous saying it, but it was true. Her voice did not even waver. She suggested the afternoon of October 15, 2013, and I agreed, writing down her address.

Before I got to the channeler's house, Master Morya appeared on the afternoon of October 14. Adhering to his advice to be still and listen, I sat in the back bedroom of the Sunny Shack, which was the designated meditation room where I taught my few yoga clients.

My eyes were shut, and I plopped cross-legged on my yoga mat when he appeared. He began energetically—not with words but in the universal language of images and sensations—leading me through an experience. Ollie rested by my side.

It started off as what I can only describe as waves of unforgiving, unrelenting forgiveness, which built in intensity and washed over my body. Then Master Morya asked aloud if I could allow forgiveness for every perceived wrong in this life and others, including all the guilt and shame I had carried for so long for simply being in a human body.

He did not ask me to ask God for forgiveness, but rather requested I allow forgiveness to roll through me. I knew internally it was unnecessary to go into the details of any so-called wrong, and I should be allowing the energy of forgiveness into my being.

It was not like the Catholic confession I had been forced to give in my teenage years. I didn't have anything to confess then, and I didn't now. Through my conversations with Sar'h, I knew already there really was no such thing as right and wrong, only experiences of the soul.

With each wave of unrelenting forgiveness that swept over my body of consciousness, my physical body felt lighter—so light, I wondered if I might be levitating, yet I did not open my eyes, which remained tightly shut in case opening them might have interrupted the experience.

Next, Master Morya asked if I wanted to be a vessel for the will of God. It wasn't what you would think. He wasn't referencing some old man in the sky and his Ten Commandments. The will of God is really a deep desire from Spirit for humans to know their own soul, to witness and experience their inner divinity. To know they are God, too. In a trance-like state, my human expression repeated over and over, "I am a vessel for the will of God."

My spine twisted clockwise in its serpent-like motion. Then I felt an overwhelming compassion for every human being, every animal, every plant, every mineral, and every single cell on planet Earth.

The movie played internally. It started with a picture of Earth from space, zooming in on the green forests and blue oceans, even down to a microscopic level. The nostalgic love I felt for every tiny bit of Earth brought me to tears, and every single cell and the spaces between the cells of my body lit up with passion to exist.

Then, in a dramatic turn, I began to deeply feel the pain and suffering of the collective human consciousness. I was taken through a historical timeline of the pain and suffering experienced by humans since the beginning of time on Earth. I realized it was a review of the collective pain body of this planet. Rape. Murder. Wars. Slavery. Witch-hunts. No stone was left unturned as I spun through time, feeling everything.

Later, I realized I felt responsible for all the pain and suffering on Earth. This is what I was allowing forgiveness for. For those of us who are 'originals'—ones who had been incarnating on earth since the 'beginning'— we often carried a guilt for every perceived wrong-doing that ever occurred. It's insane, and it runs deeper than the cellular level.

With it came the knowledge I experienced all this both as an individual soul incarnated thousands of times and as a consciousness beyond physical form. For a brief moment, I remembered I had been shown this evolution before. It was 2006, and I had been tripping on mushrooms on an Amsterdam houseboat. I realized it was one of the many times El Morya had tried to contact me over the years, and I had failed to get it. How had I missed it so many times?

El Morya then asked if I wanted to help this planet evolve. I had already answered the question in my third-grade classroom at age eight, but I answered again.

"Yes, it sounds like a hell of an adventure," I said.

Then I was shown, in the universal picture language I knew so well, the potential for the evolution of the collective human consciousness—a place and time where everyone lives in the true creative nature of the soul, rather than in his or her head, where people manifest with pure awareness—no jobs needed—and where the human concepts of suffering and scarcity of resource do not exist. This brought tears of joy to my eyes, and every cell in my body activated. *Homo luminous.*

Then I was taken back to the beginning of time, or more, so beyond time. El Morya seemed to step away from leading the experience to witnessing it. I was drawn deep into my soul, and I felt like I turned soul side out, human side in. The message came in the form of an illustrated story, like a children's book.

Souls were an energetic surge of expression from the Spirit for two purposes—to create and to experience those creations. I watched fireworks of light multiply against a dark sky. Eventually, some of the souls grew tired of creating "out there" and decided to give it a whirl on this blue-green planet called Earth. I saw a vision of 'souls in space', shooting down through a tube connecting to Earth.

The only trick was that, on most occasions, the souls forgot who they were when coming into the density of the physical body, forced to try to remember it all over again. There appeared to be no bookmark, and the soul lost its place in its own story, starting over once again in a baby's body.

These souls had the same creative abilities and the same authority to self-govern as Spirit, also known as God. Never wanting to control, govern, or impact the outcome of these souls, Spirit's only desire was to create and experience the creation, to allow the souls to realize they were creator beings as well. They were God, too.

With the images came an intense understanding Spirit, also called God or the universe, did not care about the details of our human lives. In fact, he/she/it did not give a shit, yet it was not as callous as it sounds. Rather, this creator left the souls to create and experience at will, to allow the souls to eventually understand they were the creators of their realities. They were God, too; and the 'universe' is completely indifferent to the details of our lives.

By staying neutral or even appearing uncaring to the human eye, Spirit allowed these souls to experience their inner divinity, to understand the God they sought so desperately actually existed within. The thing is even 'Spirit' doesn't really exist in the end. The universe is You. You are responsible for all your creations. There's no one out there pulling strings. There's not even a string to pull.

My soul then showed me in images and sensations, indicating a record number of human souls were beginning to feel into the chapter where they had left off. They were remembering. No longer did this human life feel like a solitary experience to them. They were realizing they had been around the human block a few hundred to a couple thousand times.

Then, in the images, I saw a million different ways to wake up, a million different ways to crack the limits of human awareness—no one way better than the other. I was shown for me it took my father's death to wake up to return to the soul's natural evolution, but it would be different for everyone.

A funny thing happened on the way to enlightenment; I lost everything, said one master to another.

I could see through the ever-shifting pictures the cracks created by human-perceived tragedies allowed waves of consciousness, or awareness, to flood in. Through the cracks in the eggshell that made up the density of human awareness, the light of the soul could seep into the physical body—

embodied consciousness.

I could see the more humans tried to resist the waves, the more lost and sick they became, often resulting in them pumping themselves full of prescription pills or insane amounts of supplements, trying to treat the sickness like I once had.

They would yell to God or the universe, why are you doing this to me, like I once had. They would give up because they felt insane and lost in the modern world, too exhausted from the rat race to continue on the soul's journey, like I once had.

In that moment of surrender, in that moment of unbelievable pain and suffering, the consciousness would roll in through the cracks, like it had for me, if they could *allow* it.

"We have to remember the act of being human is wildly courageous in and of itself." I heard the words from Sar'h so clearly. I was shown there were many souls who never dared to try human life and were watching us from the safety of their cosmic couches, some trying to give direction with no firsthand experience of what it was like to be human.

I realized there were many of us, like me, who forgot how to create outside the confines of society and the limited human mind. Many, like me, abandoned the soul in pursuit of a singular human experience, where we tended to play it safe and stay in our cages, where society told us we belonged.

Like me, many forgot human existence was actually a grand adventure in which we forget our true nature in order to have the amazing experience of realizing our divinity, remembering we are God, and reclaiming the true creator nature of our souls in this physical human form. This experience was one of the grandest adventures in all time and space, and I was on it. So were many others, and even more were ready to awaken at any moment.

After the experience was over, I was so spent I collapsed in a heap on my yoga mat. Disoriented, it took me another hour to get up. I walked my dog outside to go to the bathroom, took a steaming hot Epsom salt bath, and climbed into bed. Tomorrow I was headed to the channeler's house for a 'reading', of which I had no expectations because there wasn't anything to pull from.

11 WHAY AM I HERE, NOW?

Walking into the channeler's house, I felt instantly comfortable. After talking with her husband, I went into her office. She sat in a recliner with a digital recorder and then pulled the side lever to lie back. She tossed me a blanket, explaining it got cold when masters and archangels entered the room. I told her about my experiences over the past few weeks. She shared about when she began talking to masters at age forty. She now appeared to be in her mid-sixties, beautiful, and full of light.

The channeler said she had been in meditation when she felt every cell of her body activate, after which she was able to communicate with the unseen. Raised Baptist, she said it had been quite a shock. She mainly spoke of her relationship with Archangel Michael. Unlike ascended masters, archangels have never been in physical bodies but hold a consciousness and an interest in the evolution of Earth.

In my awakening, I naturally gravitated toward beings who knew what it was like to be human rather than ones directing from the outside, yet archangels have been so involved on Earth for so long, they tended to get human life more so than the others who weighed in with no actual experience. I—to this day—feel no strong connection to any of the archangels and feel the concept is highly misunderstood, but simply do not care.

I told her I wanted to speak to El Morya again, and I thought I had been speaking with him on my own, but my human doubts still lingered. I was so unsure of myself at the time. I had such expansive experiences, only to go back to the insecure human who consistently doubted everything. If anything, hearing this woman's story was of more comfort than anything else. She and her husband seemed to have their heads on straight. They understood business and felt grounded. They didn't wear white robes and cover themselves in crystals.

They felt like a regular couple in retirement, and yet they did not think my story was strange at all. At the time, my human self still wondered if I was crazy, and their presence gave it some much-needed relief. When we started, she seemed to go into some sort of altered state.

Like the medium, she invited my angels and guides into the room. I preferred to call them my friends or buddies. The words *angels* and *guides* were not mine. El Morya came in quickly, speaking through the channeler. He explained what I'd already understood in my childhood, adolescence, and even in India, but needed to hear again. He said if I completed what I needed to in this life, I would fully self-realize.

El Morya said after realization, souls had the choice of never incarnating back on Earth unless they wanted a specific experience. Years later, I remembered that I had, in fact, already done this. I was in the specific experience described.

El Morya—through the channel—said during my realization, I could choose whether to leave the physical body or stay in it. He implied this was a rather new choice. Most find it hard to stay in the density of the physical body, but as more masters did this, it would become easier for others.

Of course, at the time, my human expression wanted to know what I had to complete in this life to ascend while staying in the body, and it wanted it delivered in nice, neat bullet points. My soul chuckled at the thought, and he gave no steps.

"Some things we must realize on our own," a box turtle had once told a little girl. El Morya reinforced I needed to be still and listen.

"Be, be, be—not do, do, do," he said through the channel.

Once again, El Morya said others would be visiting me, and I should not be scared and should be open to what they would share. Besides being still and open, he said, most importantly, I needed to learn discernment.

Being that open would attract many visitors, both in physical and nonphysical form. I really needed to do a gut check on their intentions and determine truth for myself at the soul level. It scared me a bit, but I also understood what he was saying.

As a child playing in the backyard with various beings, I had learned, for some, fear was food. If you didn't give off fear, they would go away to feed elsewhere. I also learned at an early age not all my visitors were who they said they were, and my soul voice was the best compass in these situations.

Yet the word *discernment* was new again, and it held a certain essence of sorts I needed to sense into more. Soon after I realized the greatest place to practice my discernment was in deciphering my soul voice from the voice of the parts and pieces within me.

Which internal voice was actually Sar'h and which ones were aspects of myself which no longer served me? This proved to be a challenge I eventually mastered.

El Morya finished the session by saying I was here to assist others in their realization experiences. He said it so casually, like it was a trip to the grocery store. A bell rang inside me.

"This is what I am supposed to teach!" a voice screamed internally. "This is why I was here."

Instead of allowing the words to resonate within my being-ness, my human expression grabbed greedily at the information and twisted it all around. It saw me as some talking head, spreading wisdom in a series of lectures. My soul strongly—but gently—came in.

"Absolutely not. The way to teach realization is to be it. Gurus are obsolete in this New Energy (what comes after the New Age). The soul's or master's voice is the only guru. The kingdom is within. Remember true compassion is honoring everything and everyone as is, without trying to change it," Sar'h said energetically.

"Don't go home and start putting together PowerPoint presentations and webinars," she joked at my human's expense. "Your human self has to catch up."

I remembered El Morya showing me the pain and suffering on Earth and asking me if I wanted to help. I realized then he did not mean through activism, prayer circles, holding healing energy for Earth, or anything of the like. He only meant through self-realization.

When a human realizes who they truly are, when they realize their mastery, when they come back to the I Exist over and over and over again, the effects ripple through the rest of the world exponentially, and more so than any other action, or state of being.

There was nothing for me to do, no one for me to help. The only thing was to be and to allow the transfiguration to take place inside me. I was here to live my story rather than lecture it.

The human fought a bit—not just then but many other times. Of course, we needed to gather our swords and rally the troops. But Sar'h was no longer outside me. Her voice was rooted deep within my womb through the infusion of kundalini or spirit. Sar'h was me—the consciousness of being-ness flowing through this physical vessel of Self. I took a deep breath and relaxed. That's all there was left to do.

When I got home, I remember lying in the hammock, rocking back and forth for hours, experiencing what I can only describe as *samadhi*, a state of pure, undiluted bliss.

The sensation lasted three solid days. On the fourth day, I felt a crash beyond comparison to my drug-fueled days. I hit rock bottom and could barely get up to go to the bathroom. I couldn't stop crying, and I couldn't understand what was happening to me—the contrast in consciousness too staggering for my human to keep up.[15]

DON DRAPER: What happened to your enlightenment?
ROGER STERLING: It wore off.

---

[15] In hindsight, I learned this drop is what happens when you move from an initial "spiritual" awakening into the dark night of the soul in which all I thought I knew to be true about myself and the nature of reality was burned to the ground. For me, realization was the phoenix that rose from the ashes.

A MODERN SELF-REALIZATION STORY

—*Mad Men*, Season 5, Episode 1

Book Two: The Return to Self

When you turn the corner
And you run into yourself
Then you know that you have turned
All the corners that are left
-   Langston Hughes, Final Curve

INTRODUCTION

Now I know embodied enlightenment or realization has nothing to do with holding a Samadhi state of being, or bliss, or floating off into the sky, or walking on water, or wearing a white robe talking to your disciples, or being a billionaire, or anything external at all.

Instead, it is a messy, dirty, gritty, chaotic experience in which all you thought to be true about yourself and the nature of human life and spiritual life is burned to the ground.[16] The proverbial phoenix[17] rises from the ashes of the identities, beliefs, and ridiculous notions of what it means to be awake and spiritual have all burned to the ground, stripping you back to the original form of the I Exist.

What's left after the experience, you pick it up—knowing it is yours and yours alone—put it back on, and carry on with your life in brand new way, without questions on the nature of existence. There is no more seeking. Instead, I find personally it has become a witness in exploration to the layers of myself that continue to roll into my physical vessel. One of the funniest things of all was I went back to looking like a regular human being afterwards.

The process of self-realization always begins with the same question—

---

[16] Some call this experience the dark night of the soul and others, the Threshold, covered in the coming chapters.

[17] A phoenix is a mythological creature. Associated with the Sun, a phoenix obtains New Life by arising from the ashes of its predecessor—the singular human becomes the integrated Self in New Life, while staying in physical form.

Who Am I? In hindsight, If I had really wanted to self-realize at this moment, all I had to do was lock myself in a room and allow myself to answer this question again and again until I came to understand the true nature of existence, to allow myself to go down every rabbit hole until I came back around to the I Exist once more. All I needed was to hold myself in a room outside of time and space until I realized my one big question had no real answers but one—I Am That I Am.

Post-realization—in a state of permanent knowing I could never find myself a prisoner in the illusion of human reality again, that I would never be chained to an identity again—I read the following, and I simply love how Jed McKenna captures it in his unsentimental yet not lacking depth way of communicating.

"The fundamental conflict in the spiritual quest is that ego (the human expression) *desires* spiritual enlightenment, but ego (the human part of Self) can never *achieve* spiritual enlightenment. Self cannot achieve no self," Jed McKenna wrote in his book *Spiritual Enlightenment: The Damnedest Thing.*[18]

In other words, you have to go through the mostly painful process of understanding the human is never going to be enlightened. All you can do is allow the human to be human. The only person or thing responsible for my realization was not my ego but the unique body of wisdom individualized, Spirit individualized—in other words —my divinity—the 'I am God, too'.

McKenna continues, "Listen! Here's all you need to know to become enlightened: Sit down, shut up, and ask yourself what's true until you know. That's it. That's the whole deal; a complete teaching of enlightenment, a complete practice. If you ever have any questions or problems—the answer is always exactly the same: Sit down, shut up, and ask yourself what's true until you know. In other words, go jump off a cliff.

Don't go near the cliff and contemplate jumping off. Don't read a book about jumping off. Don't study the art and science of jumping off. Don't join a support group for jumping off. Don't write poems about jumping off. Don't kiss the ass of someone else who already jumped off. Just jump."

I could have jumped off the cliff that very day, holding up my middle finger and said, "See you bitches later!" But what kind of wise teacher would I be if I had not followed the mass into the muck, in order to have the story of telling you how I realized I was in fact, stuck in the muck, and going to show you a few ways out of it—simply by telling my story to you here.

Though, the punch line is once you realize your realization, you see clearly this is exactly what you did. Indeed, you were only pretending to be

---

[18] McKenna, Jed. *Spiritual Enlightenment: The Damnedest Thing.* Wisefool Press, 2010.

stuck in the muck and you were never really on the cliff. It's not funny until it is.

12 SOUL VERSUS SPIRITUALITY

After the glorious few blissful days floating in my hammock and subsequent drop back into the gravity of Earth, I did not know much. The one thing I did know came in the form of a sensation, rather than a thought or concept. It was not something I read in any book or learned from another. I realized there were two of me, or more. I realized this was not going to be something I could rectify in my head. It was something to feel my way through.

There was Lauren, the human expression. Her hopes and desires were on Earth. She longed for loving relationships, recognition beyond surface-level appearance, and adventure of the vacation variety. Lauren was a highly emotional human expression, who felt each and every emotion available in the human condition running deeply through her, even if it meant breaking her into pieces and dragging her in a million directions.

There was the voice of my soul, personified here by the name Sar'h. My soul really has no name—at least not one that can be typed—but here we have a story to tell. I felt, in experience of sensation, the ever-new being of my soul, containing all the wisdom of all lifetime expressions, such as Lauren. My soul felt a body of conscious wisdom, dynamically in motion.

Sure, there were many soul stories, ones I might get wrapped back into and ones that would unravel, yet something else truly special flowed from my soul — its unwavering love for, devotion to, and compassion for the human expression of self, named Lauren. A love that cannot be copied or imitated flowed from within me — inimitable.

I wondered, when I had calmed down from the latest drop into the depths of despair, who was the being who was able to distinguish between human experience and soul expression. What was this part of myself who was able to separate the human and the divine? My four-year-old experience flashed back before my vision — the I Exist. The I Am That I Am. *Aum tat sat aum.*

And, in moments of clarity, I knew the trinity of Self would merge and become one Self in a new human form, yet my human condition would not allow me, at the time, to see how I could move toward this perceived goal of the human, soul, and I Am becoming one.

I did not yet realize I needed to lean back into the experience, so I took up with what I did know. I knew I had a soul voice, one that sang a song for me and me alone. I knew it was a love song. I realized the next step included allowing my human expression to trust my soul voice unwaveringly and to allow the undiluted love the soul expresses for the human to flow like a fountain within me. By allowing the unconditional love from the fountain within to merge with the human expression's trust of the wisdom within, I created the bridge joining the two as one—'I Am' as my witness.

I knew without words any and all suffering I experienced in these moments—ones I refer to as 'the back and forth' from expansion in awareness to constriction within the cage of human identity—came from the perceived separation between my humanity and my divinity—between Lauren and Sar'h.

Without knowing what to do, I decided with every fiber of my being-ness to follow my soul voice blindly into the void. It felt like sitting in a dark empty room, allowing my eyes to slowly adjust to the midnight within me as I made the Return to Self. And, as my eyes adjusted to the darkness, I found while it seemed I was making my way back to Self, I really never left it. The room was not empty, I simply had not felt its contents, or essence, yet. I was not yet able to feel myself in its entirety.

The first notion appeared to me on those crucial days in the hammock. It was simple—the soul always speaks simply, and the message was *solvitur ambulando*—it is solved by walking. I knew I had a million miles to go, and yet one step is all it would take.

This room outside of time and space I spoke of, to examine the question—Who Am I?—was going to be a room in motion making its way around planet Earth, and expand into the cosmos, on occasion, for picked up parts and pieces of myself way out there too.

From 2013 to 2015, any experiences of diving deeper into the Return to Self were not the result of any teachings, classes, books, or mentors. Further, deeper into Self, was only 'achieved' by listening to the hum of the song of my soul and following it wherever it went.

While El Morya appeared to me at various junctures in my journey, he was not there to teach me anything. Beyond the three things he told me through the medium and the channel, he rarely interjected his thoughts or ideas into my life.

El Morya simply showed up in critical moments, sometimes smiling, sometimes ridiculously serious; he only stood to remind me who I was and why I was here in this amazing lifetime expression. Like any teachers worth their weight in gold, he showed me where to look inside, not what to see. His presence was a lighthouse on the shore of a foggy sea. I steered the boat, but every now and again, he would shine a beam on the zig zag path beyond any concept linear time and space, and only within me in—in the Return to Self that is realization.

Sar'h and I inspired a few on our walk around the world, and we were certainly inspired by others, but our pilgrimage was a journey back to Self—that was the real classroom. *Homo viator*—human on a voyage. One does not need to leave their couch to make that journey, occurring beyond time and space; they only need to connect with the body of wisdom within.

At one point, I did take a few detours from my soul path to explore the collective spiritual consciousness, mainly the New Age. What I sought in these New Age realities was a human desire to share my experiences and reinforce the path I was on, to remind my human self I was not crazy, yet what I found in these realities or in the collective spiritual consciousness was quite disturbing and not at all comforting.

I realized rather quickly spirituality has absolutely nothing—zero—to deal with embodied enlightenment, or self-realization. I wasn't quite sure what the spiritual people sought. Cosmic experiences, magic solutions, power, ways to make money off people in their victimhood, unattainable perfection of the human condition. There were no answers for me here in the New Age, just like there were no answers for me in the yogic philosophies of yore.

The spiritual world offered nothing for my Return to Self—other than a somewhat entertaining distraction and a deep and constant reminder all answers were inside of me, not in a New Age workshop.

I found my short journey through the New Age to be a huge waste of time and energy, not to mention money. I don't want to waste precious pages in my book on this, for there is too much wisdom to share to waste space on the ridiculous.

However, I provided a few examples of spiritual distractions, simply because anyone desiring realization really must walk on by these circus tents, rather than walking into them and setting up camp. Lifetimes can be wasted tangling yourself in antiquated spiritual teachings.

Thus, for the sake of example, one great big detour happened when I met a woman in Peru, a lovely woman but full on stuck in the New Age loop — one that has no exit. One night in a hushed tone in her hotel room, she told me about a strange belief from the New Age schools of thought called twin flames — a wonderful fairy tale in which you met your twin soul and achieved enlightenment together. Too funny.

It provided a nice distraction for me for a few months before I realized I was my own twin flame. My soul and my human as one. The experience did serve because once I was done with my exploration of this crazy concept, I was dropped right back into the unwavering, undiluted love the soul has for me, the human expression of self, that needs nothing from outside of itself.

Another woman I ran into insisted I had to take a class from a dude who taught you how to access what he called the tiny space of the heart. Interested, I went out to Sedona to take his course, and read his books which were, of course, required. I never got through the mumbo jumbo in these dense texts. While realization is the most simple and natural of experiences, spirituality is ridiculously complex and burdensome—a way to wear oneself out in the search for the proverbial truth.

Anyone spending months working their chakras, memorizing the healing properties of crystals or the words of complicated decrees, going through a never-ending series of initiations and activations, or consulting their guides and angels—without understanding the nature of sovereignty and their own soul's voice—they are not only delaying their realization experience, they are putting up a barricade to it—a wall between human and soul self. I didn't know much, yet I knew the difference between intellect and wisdom, between thought-based emotions and deep feeling. My soul showed me to get where I was going—further into Self—wisdom and deep feeling marked the only way to arrive.

There, in Sedona, this mystical teacher stood on stage and told us this was his first time on Earth, and he walked into the body he now inhabited. Thus, I knew instantly he offered nothing about realization. Self-realization is really reserved for those coming to the conclusion of their life reincarnation cycle on Earth. Most souls, in a linear view, for the sake of writing, incarnate between one thousand to two thousand times until they reach the point in time and space that is the designated lifetime for mastery, when all the wisdom from all lifetimes and in between lives comes home to Self in a fully integrated body of consciousness.

A lot of these 'teachers' out there who claimed to be first-lifers or walk-ins have some kernel of consciousness to share because they came from a place without the duality, gravity, and linearity that lies naturally upon someone who finds themselves within in many experiences and incarnations. On a good day, they can remind us of the illusion of maya. On a bad day, they will empty your wallet and convince you the path to salvation is complicated and requires you to do it in a certain way that is not uniquely yours, without actually having experienced it for themselves. In other words, what these so-called teachers offered was a reminder there were realities that existed beyond duality, linearity, and gravity—if even that.

Having never gone through the self-realization experience themselves, often what they bring to the table is a view from 'star people' who love to watch Earth from their lazy cosmic couches, never having actually inhabited a human body or experience but offering tons of useless, not to mention expensive advice—that is, if your desired experience is self-realization. If you just want to get wacky in the New Age and have a metaphysical experience or two and skip the whole realization thing, this is probably your guy.

During this time, I also met many people who said they were not from Earth and here on assignment or a mission from planet or star xxx, which actually held some truth to it. But Earth is a funny place, you don't just visit once and go 'home.' This used to make me cry, until I severed the tiny final thread connecting me to some long off star family, in which I experienced in an off-planet life.

By 'signing up' to come to Earth and incarnating as human, I realized for myself, you actually release an idea of external home and home then becomes Self, as you make the wild and amazing journey to a self-realized human being, throughout many lifetimes, until the reincarnation cycle comes to a close. Home is now you, in all your grand sovereignty.

I never bothered to tell these people I met this fact—why burst their bubbles—but I knew from personal experience once a soul came to Earth, basically, they reincarnated over and over again until home becomes Self. They never went home back to planet or star xxx; or if they did, it would never be home again. Sorry, you're human and not at all special or exceptional. None of us are.

This dude had a rock star-like following. People would line up for autographs and pictures during the breaks and it made me throw up in my mouth a little. Another externalization of wisdom, of the divine. It was so simple. The kingdom everyone is looking for is within. As soon as the divine is externalized, it created a dead end instantly.

The thing with these teachers, there was always a little kernel of truth or wisdom, which kept people tied to their every word. He offered a way to access the divinity within, but through a series of complicated steps, which included 'stimulating the clitoris on the roof of the mouth with the tongue while crossing your eyes.' No kidding! He went over and over the steps in a PowerPoint presentation, with people asking the same questions over and over again.

"Got to get the steps right or I won't be spiritual enough." I heard their thoughts.

I wanted to stand on my chair and yell, "CLOSE YOUR EYES. TAKE A DEEP BREATH. LISTEN TO THE SONG OF YOUR SOUL. THAT IS IT. THAT IS ALL."

I never did.

At the lunch breaks in this workshop with the walk-in, people would "charge" their vegan, gluten-free meals with their hands preparing it for their sacred consumption. I found one friend and off we went to get beers and sacred sushi, and immediately shoveled it into our mouths.

Everything is sacred and nothing is. Self-realization is what happens when you are relaxed and having fun, not in adhering to strict rules and diets. If you really want to renounce something, don't give up food and material possessions. Instead renounce your attachments to old spiritual identities; renounce the continuously repeating pattern to place your divinity into something external; renounce being tied to the notion you must be perceived externally as spiritual or conscious to allow your own self-realization; renounce—above all—the notion you must spiritually perfect yourself.

The cool thing was when I was in Sedona for this ridiculousness, I met a man who was a professional psychologist, specializing in assisting people with bringing previous life experiences back to Self for integration. I knew I could do this on my own, but I felt it would be helpful for someone hold space for me as I brought back an especially difficult one. There in Sedona I went to his house.

Respected by a peer in consciousness and safe, I walked this previous lifetime back home. At the end of our session, this man said, "Wow. I didn't have to do anything. You did it yourself."

"Of course, I did," I said. "Do other people show up and expect you to do this for them?"

The notion seemed absurd to me.

"All the time," he said, as he gave me a hug before I walked out the door.

Blissfully clueless in the New Age world, I did not know anyone would place their power in the hands of someone else, willingly—and while paying them. I didn't know much at the time, yet I knew enough to know I simply needed someone to be a sovereign support during this intense experience.

I realized as I reversed my car down the man's driveway most of the people who came to him were expecting him to fix whatever issue was plaguing theirs lives, rather than taking responsibility for themselves. I knew if someone else fixed something for me, the results will never stick. I knew I had to do it by myself and for myself alone. I also knew rather than fixing or healing anything, I could only allow the parts and pieces of Self to integrate, if there was going to be lasting result for my human experience.

Quick pause here to define integration versus releasing. Integration, by definition, is combining one or more things with another, and in doing so, becoming whole. In bringing in a wounded story from an old lifetime for integration — which is simply done through becoming aware of its presence without needing to know the details — that old lifetime story or wound becomes whole within the body of conscious wisdom that is the soul. It's hard to put words to this energetic experience that is so simple, yet wordless because it happens beyond the mind in most cases.

Releasing is to allow something to flow freely. The choice on whether to release or integrate, or to not even care about it, is always up to the discernment of a person's unique soul voice. However, I personally found when I released something from the human perspective it continued to live on and come back and mess with me. For example, feeling the old wounds of persecution from a previous life continuously, which had nothing to do with my current reality.

If I integrated something, the wisdom from the experience distilled, meaning... through pure awareness.... whatever I learned from an experience was woven into the tapestry of Self... yet the old stories of right and wrong, of victim and perpetrator were completely dissolved in the process.

In one perception, distillation of wisdom simply filters out any duality—or any illusion of maya—from an experience, and leaves only the wisdom obtained from the experience—without the story, without attachment to the old identity.

Even later, in my expanded consciousness, I felt this man was worth every penny of the two hundred and fifty dollars I handed him when I was done. That's why when people are ready to take full responsibility of their life, yet still desire someone to come walk by them for a little while on their path, I'm happy to do it. I now understand deeply the importance of the energetic exchange in this experience, which usually takes the form of a monetary gift.

It is not a business for me, for I would not see anyone who wishes to come to me for multiple visits, or anyone expecting me to give answers or fixes for their perceived human problems. There is one, maybe two times, I might meet with someone and then it is time to move on and find what is true and real for themselves. And maybe as I walk beside them, I can show someone the door to space where problems dissolve, where the illusion is lifted, yet they must walk into that space alone.

Most of these New Age practitioners will take your money for years and years until it runs dry, always offering the latest "new" thing. The thing is there is nothing "new" in realization. It is a story as old as time itself.

Looking back, in sum, I mainly spent the two years here, focused upon my soul-level experiences—on the experiences reclaiming, integrating the parts and pieces of the history of myself, scattered all over the globe.

The really interesting thing—as I gathered the parts and pieces of Self, I felt my history, the old stories I had told myself for eons, changing and evolving in every other lifetime I held, not just this one.

For example, in the lifetime in which I had taken my own life—once I integrated that part of myself, once I brought that old story and identity of Self back home—the story shifted and I, in fact, never went through that experience.

For me, this is the true healing, and it had nothing to do with my chakras, energetic balancing, or help from any angels or guides. What I learned, the wound doesn't stop being a wound; however, I stopped perceiving it as a wound, as something I needed to heal—the transmutation occurring in the soul's distillation of wisdom—through integration.

In the end, once in the realized state, problems don't disappear, yet there is the inability to perceive a problem as a problem. I am no longer stuck in the cage of a fixed, static human identity. The fixed identity in a fixed reality is what keeps people stuck in the cage. And when you step out of the cage —it feels somewhat like death, but more so like freedom— perhaps they are the same thing in a way.

For me, this marked the permanence of the self-realized state of being —I stopped working on myself. I stopped perceiving myself as stuck in a singular reality or a fixed identity. Instead, I allowed Self, and nothing more. I allowed myself to move freely within multiple realities. I allowed myself to be in the perpetual state of becoming, permanently yet dynamically, without any attachment to my human identity or any perception of a fixed reality or any perception of a divide between my humanity and my divinity. In this new space, I became a New Energy being, able to sovereignly create my own reality, in any point of existence.

13 PICKING UP PARTS AND PIECES OF SELF

At times, this period in my life felt like a scavenger hunt for a million-piece puzzle I turned upside down and scattered all over Earth. I was a human desperately trying to feel whole. As soon as I would get to one place, I'd find a clue for another.

El Camino del Corazón (the path of the heart) in Peru led me to Sedona in Arizona. Next, I found myself in the King's Chamber of the Great Pyramid in Cairo, floating down the Nile on a sailboat, flying to Petra in Jordan, and soaking in the Dead Sea.

A suicide bomber missed me by a mile in Mount Sinai, where I picked up a lifetime that seemed to continue on long after I left the physical form. In this lifetime, I played the role of martyr, and this experience continuously bled into my current reality. I made the arduous trek out to a deserted Mount Sinai hotel to reel this lifetime back in—to bring it back home within Self—for she had been 'out there' reliving—in a never-ending loop—an old story of persecution more than two thousand years.

Sar'h and I volunteered with sea turtles in Costa Rica, walking and talking with Yeshua down its coastline. Yeshua, and others like Babaji, seemed to make rounds in visiting me, reminding me of certain aspects of this journey home. Sometimes it got to be so much I asked them to go away. I'd love to publish my writing about these visits one day but find it too distracting here, where I really want to talk about the most important connection you can make—the one with Self.

With my disembodied friends, I climbed ruins in Mexico, where I let go of the need for recognition. I let go of the need to be seen as some sort of spiritual teacher who needs to be followed and adored. It was an energetic experience of moving beyond ego in sharing my journey of consciousness— in this incarnation—and I'm not sure why this happened in a pyramid in the middle of a jungle. Yet that was part of the fun making in this part of my life. Each day I went through another death, so why not do it on vacation instead of stuck on the couch for yet another miserable day of integration.

Together, my crew and I whirled like a hurricane across the Philippines, where I learned how to play again on Earth. We swam with dolphins in Hawaii, who taught me of the joy that is love beyond duality and conditions. We rode horses in Spain and explored medieval villages we'd once lived in. Finally, Sar'h led me to southern France in Spring of

2015, the home of the Magdalene energies, and the grand finale of our world tour. It was a trip that nearly physically killed me as the integrations of these lifetimes were beyond intense. Sar'h decided to tell this particular story from her perspective in a later chapter.

After this trip, I came to the understanding the human expression of me was not in charge of gathering the puzzle pieces. That would take another five hundred lifetimes. Although it had been an amazing experience to fly around the world on a grand search for Self, I shifted in perspective to knowing the soul was really in charge of this experience, this distillation of wisdom from all lifetimes. My soul showed me—the human, the ego—it was time to allow these parts and pieces to come home naturally. All I had to do was relax.

The experience took several months once I returned to my home and retired to my bed, sleeping sometimes seventeen hours a day. Sometimes it was physically painful. Other times it was emotionally draining. More times than not, I watched myself, or my human identities rather, die over again and again, only to find I still woke up the morning.

If my mind became involved in it, it would cause the broken record in my head to make me want to drive off a cliff in my truck. Sometimes I'd yell, "I can't take it anymore, soul. Pull over and let me jump out of the car!" But the only way out was through. Driving off a cliff, I knew I'd end up back in a baby's body again and again until I allowed my realization to take place.

I did find on occasion I held the ability to hit pause, take a break, go to a bar with my friends and throw back a few shots, and dance until the sun came up. But a pause was all I got—for there was no going back, once the realization experience began. I could not un-see what I saw in my awakening, of learning I was in the cage ordering off the limited human menu.

Realization, at its core, was a complete annihilation of who I thought I was and an obliteration of my human identity—one that brought me to my knees over and over again, humbled me in ways you could never imagine, and then, when I couldn't take one second of it more, it dumped me into an unfathomable stream of pure existence.

When I was really ready to be done with this whole intensely uncomfortable experience of integrating the parts and pieces of myself, I packed up my truck with camping gear and my dog, and off we went to the Palo Duro Canyon State Park in Texas. It was fall in the Texas Panhandle — linear year 2015. I set up my tent in a lonely section of the canyon and said out loud, hands raised to the blue cloudless sky above me, "Okay, let's get this done. Everyone—all parts and pieces of myself—it is time to come Home—NOW!"

The next few nights I rolled around in my sleeping bag, in and out of consciousness. I felt the faces of many expressions, many human lifetimes come into my vessel, through my physical back. Sometimes I might see an image or a face of these previous incarnations, or aspects of Self. Sometimes I felt an emotion from one as if it were my own, but I knew it wasn't mine.

In this case, I didn't know any of the stories of the aspects of Self making their way home. Before I held detailed awareness of each lifetime brought home. Some details felt important to know, and now my soul showed me it was not. Plus, I was too tired to care, and the details did not matter. I realized I was not my previous lives anymore. I was none of the old rogue identities. I was Lauren, a souled being in physical form, and we—all of us—were going to walk into something new without having to analyze, describe, heal, fix, re-write—none of it. I was done!

In some ways, in this intense and physically and emotionally painful experience, I felt I made my soul a bucket of distillation and commanded all these rogue aspect identities to go into said bucket. I don't know if it's the best way to do such a thing—in fact I would not advocate for it—yet it was my way, so I write it here.[19]

Now, of course, after this trip, an aspect or piece of myself would return, yet it was never a big deal henceforth. I knew exactly what was occurring, and with no resistance, the integration happened rather quickly.

El Morya told me even in mastery, parts and pieces returned in a state of being—the perpetual state of becoming. Yet, it is something that is beautifully sensual, once your tie, or attachment to, a fixed, static human identity is laid to rest in the realization experience. I found it to be true to my current reality.

Further, I found my secret formula that contains no magic, only consciousness. I found after long brisk walk, a hot salt bath, and a few good night's sleep, whatever needed to take place did as parts and pieces of Self trickled in for distillation. I could tell you my human expression started to trust this whole experience, but rather—at this point—I know it was just too tired to care, and in my surrender, the trust rolled in.

The human Lauren did the only thing left to do. She took a deep breath and relaxed. And that truly is when the consciousness rolled in, in a really real and permanent way. This deep and conscious breath marked, for me, the point in which I really moved from the shallow end of spiritual understanding to the depths of the ocean of my own inimitable

---

[19] This is where the disclaimers come into play. Please make sure you have read them completely and agree to them completely. If you start this kind of process within yourself before you are ready, it will send you to the mad house. I do not give recommendations. I only share my story.

consciousness.

Then, the next clue from my soul came up for inspection—something new to ponder. Further—Sar'h, my soul, showed me instead of moving toward realization like a goal or a finish line, we needed instead to reverse our vehicle, our body of consciousness or the universe of Self, back into the parking space of self-realization—a state of realization which always existed.

"It certainly wasn't going to be boring." My 'big I self' told my 'little I self' this a lot. It was the way of comforting the human who really wanted to be human—to find a boyfriend, acquire more friends, fit in, be successful in the eyes of their peers, get involved in the soap opera of life once again, and all the stuff humans like to do. Experience, experience, experience—over and over again, in a fixed form of identity, which created the illusion that was the barred cage, the crystal prison, and the limited menu of life in the collective human consciousness.

My soul would dangle a carrot before the human, saying there is so much more; don't you want to find out about it. And my 'little I self' would set down those distractions like boys and success and dramas again, once more, focusing on our destiny—the only true destination of human beings on Earth—the state of being that is realization.

Destiny comes from the Latin *to make firm*; and my deepest soul desire was not only to experience the realized state and leave Earth yet again—it was to stay here on Earth, to make firm my home, my sovereign kingdom, within my physical form.

14 SAR'H'S STORY

For Lauren, it started in Southern France in the Spring of 2015, when she began to remember key lifetimes that all came together in this one point, this unique lifetime. On this trip and what came after, she began to remember the distilled wisdom from several lifetimes, key points in our collective consciousness of Self, some two thousand years ago and further back to the beginning of life on Earth in a civilization called Atlantis. Here is my story, that of Sar'h, or Sa'Ra.

In Alexandria, Egypt, when the time switched from BC to AD, I was born awake to a sad mother whose partner had been nailed to a cross months earlier. It was a play that had to be acted out, I learned, to demonstrate the kingdom was within, to tell the nature of a conscious life eternal through a dramatic story a human could understand—or not.

Some of those around me could hold this awareness without diving into the grief. Others got lost in their grief, and let themselves loose in the emotion of anger. For it is easier to be angry than sad. It is often easier to grab a pitchfork, than lie it down and let it go.

We lived among underground corridors, dark and damp hallways that ran beneath the bustling metropolis above our hiding places. The dank smell of mold and feces was covered up by a variety of scents and spices.

Frankincense and myrrh, juniper and cloves. I could tell the people around me were waiting for me to grow up a little before we left. Men visited with coded news and food supplies. My mother was a busy woman, respected by her peers, and a leader of sorts. I was placed in the care of many others who lived beneath the ground with us in hiding.

One day I watched my mother's face change from peace and adoration to horror and fear. Another woman was holding me. She was in a space of great turmoil. My mother saw I absorbed all the pain and suffering from this woman, taking it on as my own, and she snatched me quickly back into her own arms. That's when I knew and I started to remember who I was and why I found myself back in a physical body on Earth. It was not for the words I seldom spoke; but for the consciousness, flowing through my body and being.

One day—I must have been three or four years old—we made our escape. Those living underground with us had packed our bags. Now we ran under the fresh air of the night sky to a boat at the docks. I noticed the constellations above me formed a line. Everyone around me appeared nervous, on edge. The sun was starting to come up over the horizon. I did not speak much, but I never spoke much at all anyway—a life of silence.

When we arrived at the boat, the men with us noticed the sails of the ship had been tattered and torn, but there was no turning back; we had to go now. As we moved further and further away from shore, the collective relief of having made a getaway from a persecuted life in Egypt was replaced by the sinking notion we might not make it across the Mediterranean Sea to our new home among the forest and tree people who lived there.

The people on the boat gathered in prayer, meditation, deep concentration without thought. I watched as they each collected their being-ness within to keep themselves from dropping over that oh-so-tempting edge that led only to despair.

What we needed was wind, from a certain direction, and a lot of it to make up for the poor shape of the sails. I remember it was a long journey, with many ups and downs. The world was a cruel and ridged place then. You could be killed for speaking a single word. Persecuted for your bloodline. Raped for simply existing in female form.

Consciousness was but a single spark in a dark, dark world. With all the food gone, dirt-covered in tattered clothes, we arrived to the shore of what is now called France, in a port that is now called Saintes-Marie-de-la-Mer.

There are a copious number of stories out there about the children of Yeshua and Mary Magdalene. I find all of them to be true, for all that a story needs to be true is to have someone believe in it. There's no need to defend or correct truth anymore.

There's no need to educate anyone on the true teachings of Yeshua, or Mary Magdalene, or of anyone incarnated at this time and space on Earth. As soon as you have picked up the sword of defensiveness, you have missed the heart of what Yeshua and Mary Magdalene and crew taught.

What was actually important was we, as a collective Christ consciousness inhabiting physical form, laid the groundwork for, and established the lines of consciousness, we set forth back in our lives in Atlantis, for something we called 'usara'.

Usara was not a word but a song sung 'ooo-saaar-raaaahhhh.' It was the song of Spirit embodied, a song of bringing the divine into our human vessels, our physical bodies. It was a dream one day we would be able to access New Life, in which we could experience the deathless, birth-less nature of the soul in a physical form on Earth. A state of knowing the kingdom was within, while retaining our physical experience in human form.

In this lifetime from the switch from BC to AD, I lived out the rest of my days in Gaul, or France, with a Celtic tribal community, or the Druids, as some call them now. My mother retreated to allow what we called then ascension, for it was much too hard to stay in physical form after one became whole, human and divine combined.

I hugged her goodbye when I was no more than ten years old. My life was marked by constant hiding, endless physical deaths of those around me at the hands of the elements or Roman soldiers, *and* the celebration of life that lives on with no physical body—eternal life free of and beyond physical form. There's really not much more to it.

The others, the ones who stayed back in our homelands or who had moved into other parts of Europe merging with like-consciousness communities, liked to argue over what Yeshua said or didn't say and what it meant or didn't mean. Yet, deeper than their arguments rolled the birth of a consciousness taking root in Earth today—something I honor deeply.

I could feel them always in my multiplicity of Self and often visited these people in their secret meetings, in what some might call an *astral body*. One group signaled when their secret night meetings occurred to each other by wearing a crimson-colored scarf while out in the towns nearby. Many of these souls incarnated again now and have a physical group on Earth presently called the Crimson Circle with an angelic council counterpart called the Crimson Council.

These people called themselves shaumbra, which means a soul family that is on a journey together. Together they bring not only the Christ consciousness but also the breath of New Life to the planet at this time in which the New Energy grows roots with Earth's soil. I shared all of this with Lauren as she prepared to meet these people in her physical life in the coming year.

After the crucifixion, few of the followers of Yeshua actually understood what we all were doing here and what Yeshua's life meant for the evolution of Earth. It used to make me very angry to know they fought so much among themselves; that they twisted Yeshua's words around and used them against each other.

"No, he said this. Not that. You don't get it," they yacked back and forth.

We had enough enemies, hiding behind every corner, so why all this fighting internally, I wondered. Eventually, I found I could not care about these people and their internal fights anymore, though I could honor them greatly from the soul perspective, from the expanded view of the evolution of Earth and humanity.

Sometimes you realize there is nothing to win, and everything is lost by staying in the endless argument that is right and wrong. Sometimes the best way to love is to leave, to walk away. I love the Rumi poem, which will say this so much better than I ever could:

> Out beyond ideas of wrongdoing
> and rightdoing there is a field.
> I'll meet you there.
> When the soul lies down in that grass
> the world is too full to talk about.

This poem could stop everything worldly dualistic in its tracks—all the wars, hate, violence, fights over the 'truth.' Yet, only the people with eyes can see it; only the ones with ears will hear it. And I had to let it go once again.

I felt my soul, or the consciousness I carried, I wasn't really sure which one it was or if I contained both. It didn't matter, my need to have a physical vessel for the consciousness to flow through on Earth had come to an end.

With little fanfare nor flashes of bright lights, among my adopted family and friends, my body returned to the Earth and my consciousness flowed free in the orgasmic release that is death. Even in death my human heart— where my humanity and divinity met as one—lay heavy yet hopeful.

For centuries, so many people would die in the name of Yeshua's teachings, in the defense of the crazy concepts of right and wrong, and in the quest for the holy grail. Many of the crimson scarf people, the shaumbra, returned for lifetimes as Cathars or playing roles in the Knights Templar. More swords; less souls lying down in the grass beyond the fields of right and wrong.

I, as a consciousness, branched off of this group at this portion in linear time, choosing instead to immerse myself in human life and all it had to offer. I held many lives in many times, knowing there was no such thing as good or bad, only experience, but I return to tell you of three lives now for it has bigger implications for those choosing embodiment—realization while staying in physical form—for that was the Atlantean dream, and the consciousness laid through the work of Yeshua and the family of souls surrounding him.

The Atlantean dream, which was sung in the temples of Atlantis, was simply an invitation, a knowingness, that one day souls would open to the ability to bring their divinity into physical form and stay on Earth, even just for a little bit. For the consciousness of Sar'h embodied as Lauren, together we knew we would stay not just for a little while but decades longer—however long it took to root.

Sar'h (pronounced saa- raa)—my given name in this life was Hebrew, but was also based on the Atlantean song that was sung, for it was our dream one day we would be able to live in our bodies and bring our divinity into them, while remaining on Earth. What comes beyond that is a new book, a new chapter of Life, one each of us are sovereignly writing as we go along.

Yeshua and friends showed this with his dramatic play—death and resurrection. Not a souled being, Yeshua was a consciousness created by you and me in our Atlantean lifetimes—a lifetime that seemed to go so wrong.

The funniest part of the play, of being a 'child' of Yeshua and Mary Magdalene, was simply that it was a story to show what was birthed by their union on Earth. The child truly born through the union of Yeshua and Mary Magdalene was not a human being but a consciousness, the possibility of this New Life described above. Many would return again, even and especially the crimson scarf-wearing folks who called themselves shaumbra would return, and we would try again when the New Age turned into New Energy.

All that is born, all that is created, all the elements of nature are interwoven and united with each other. All that is composed shall be decomposed; everything returns to its roots; matter returns to the origins of matter. —Gospel of Mary Magdalene[20]

I, Sar'h, ask you to close your eyes and open your heart to the Atlantean experience, the dream. Shoot back to before things got so very messed up, when you and I had a dream one day there would be life with no death, that we would know and live with the wisdom that we were the creators of our reality — along with others who knew themselves to be God, too. We would not simply realize during and after our physical death when our souls moved beyond the veil, but the veil would be lifted while we stayed in physical form.

There was a song we sang—the vibrational frequency of the life of a creator embodied—it went oooooo —saaaaaaaah—raaaaaaah—and what it meant in simple terms was Spirit embodied and so much more than cannot be put in words.

When Lauren began to name her book and publication series, I handed her the title—Becoming Sar'h—pronounced Saaaaaaa-Raaaaaaa.

---

[20] Leloup, Jean-Yves. The Gospel of Mary Magdalene. Rochester, Vermont: Inner Traditions Bear & Company, 2002.

Lauren knew what it meant deep within the caverns of her being, but we could not tell you in words until now. A tipping point had to be reached. Becoming New Life.

If you felt drawn to this book or to Lauren's writing, holding this consciousness of usara, perhaps you were there in Atlantis singing this song of New Life, too. Perhaps, you came to have a gentle nudge into remembering what you came to sovereignly create this round, in this designated lifetime.

I want to state it again. In another way, for those of you with the Yeshua and Mary Magdalene connection in addition to Atlantis, this concept was introduced once again through the play, the act of consciousness, enacted during this time.

The mythical and magical child called Sar'h—the holy grail—all the stories and interpretations of this history, which are all true because they are made so by belief, all lead up to what was truly birthed—the potential for New Life or Embodied Enlightenment. Embodied Creation.

What was really making its way across the Mediterranean Sea on the dilapidated sail boat, was not any child or human being, it was the consciousness of being, of knowing yourself as God. The song of Saaa- Raa was making its way from the East to the West, the internalization of the divine. The song of Saaa-Raa is a song of the state of no separation in which the lines between human and divine dissolve, in which the wall between our physical and etheric world comes tumbling down.

It matters not whether a biological child was born, if my soul was in that body or not. What matters now is I allow myself—Lauren and Sar'h as one being—in total joy to be a vessel for the consciousness of New Life, of the song of Saa-Raa to flow through me, in creation of a slip stream for those choosing consciousness over automation for eons to come.

This may only make sense to a few, but for those who know, the song of New Life flows un-diluted through your embodied vessel in this very special lifetime in which the experience is beyond love, beyond joy, and beyond anything our human parts and pieces can even imagine. If realization plain and simple is all you seek, do read on, for this book contains this story as well, beyond the crimson edges of the next chapter.

15 THE CRIMSON YEARS

FEBRUARY 2015—SEPTEMBER 2018

Here, in this chapter, I, Lauren, am only briefly sharing a few experiences with my time at the Crimson Circle organization. This is by no means an overview of the organization in full. I am definitely not, nor have I ever been affiliated with or employed by the Crimson Circle organization. I experienced these materials only as a member of its audience. I encourage you to check out the website at www.crimsoncircle.com for their official information and history, written by shaumbra and for shaumbra, for I am not one.

In February 2015, I was in Spain visiting my then boyfriend when he pulled out his computer and announced enthusiastically we were going to watch a shoud.
"What is a shoud?" I asked.
He responded it was a monthly online gathering for an organization called the Crimson Circle, in which a man named Geoffrey Hoppe channeled a being named Adamus St. Germain.
I rolled my eyes, "Here we go, more channeled information."
Yet, in the first few minutes of this online gathering I knew there was something truly special in it for me. Adamus, my new friend in this life, basically said in this channel—people hit the glass ceiling[21] on God by externalizing it.
It marked the first time anything spiritually or consciously presented to me externally matched my insides, and it was amazing. Fireworks went off inside of my soul, and I knew I would fall in love with this group of amazing souls.
Adamus said in the shoud, in hitting the glass ceiling on God,

---

[21] In America, there is a concept called the glass ceiling. It was first used in the 1980s to describe an intangible barrier within a hierarchy, preventing women and/or minorities from obtaining upper-level, or leadership, positions in the workforce. In this context, hitting the glass ceiling on God refers to the barrier created in the externalization of God, which keeps you from the experience of internally knowing yourself as "God, also." A term also used by Tobias channeled via Geoffrey Hoppe.

humanity created an invisible barrier in which they could not expand into knowing themselves as God, too—as God internal.

He described how this artificial ceiling kept things held in and restricted people from expansion, by mistaking mass consciousness[22] for God and vigorously holding onto and defending an external concept of God that does not exist—a God that humans place above and outside of themselves.

Adamus said instead of putting God out there in the unknown, he said this group, called shaumbra, held the ability to place God right in here inside themselves. He said something I already knew to be true for myself. He said we could put the consciousness of Spirit, Source, the I Am, the I Exist, right here inside of each of us.

"That's what embodied enlightenment is about. Not the consciousness of a God out there or a creator out there, but right here. Sounds so simple. It is. It's just … yeah," he added.[23]

Soon in 2017, I had my own 'I am God, too' experience, but right then, it still hung within my body of awareness as a concept placed there for my soul to examine. For the next two to three years, I took any and all courses and workshops offered by the Crimson Circle, opening my heart fully as well as my wallet, and I was happy to do so until I wasn't. I didn't learn anything my soul was not going to show me on my own. However, the greatest benefit I received from the materials is my human expression of Self came to understand fully and completely, each and everything that happened in the natural phenomena that is the Return to Self, or self-realization.

In other words, these courses and materials offered by the Crimson Circle supported an experience in which my humanity was able to meet my divinity in consciousness, or awareness, of why I stood here on this Earth once again. I continue to be forever grateful for the experiences I went through with myself through the materials and events as well the meeting of old friends from my days back in Atlantis, during the time of Yeshua, and beyond.

I took the Sexual Energy School, which reinforced my soul experiences teaching me I never needed to beg, borrow, or steal energy. It was an experience, in which I reinforced my prior knowingness energy was an abundant resource that flowed within my consciousness and responded to the song of my own soul. There was an online class called Aspectology[24]

22 Mass consciousness, or the collective human consciousness, is a collection of shared beliefs, ideas, and moral attitudes which operate as a unifying force within Earth's global society.

23 The Kharisma Series, Shoud 6: "Kharisma 6" — Featuring Adamus, channeled by Geoffrey Hoppe. Presented to the Crimson Circle on February 7, 2015.

that was all about picking up parts and pieces of Self, as I have written about in the previous chapters. I experienced my own version of the materials without having watched the program until much later, yet it did help me put words to experience in hindsight.

Yet, for some of the people in this new community I found myself in, instead of taking these materials and weaving them into their space of internal knowing, they used it against each other. When they fought, they would point at each other and say, "You have the sexual energy virus. You are feeding off me." It was the conscious version of the cooties, this virus of energy feeding that was covered in the Sexual Energy School. Yet, the only way people could feed off of you was if you let them, and the only way you let them was if you were still feeding on your own Self, internally.

If someone behaved erratically, which is often the case when moving into realization—it's a real crazy making experience—a so-called friend might yell, "Your aspects are showing," as they mocked and pointed their accusing finger at another. In this new world, in addition to feeling like I was running from the virus cooties on a playground, I also felt as if I was back in the age of Yeshua, yet instead of fighting over what Yeshua said or didn't say, they fought over what Adamus said or didn't say.

Adamus quotes were thrown around like swords and daggers, and I felt like I was constantly dodging them. It felt like a war zone, and I often retreated to a bomb shelter I created within my own soul until I said, "No more!"

I did come to understand—when I dug deeper—that the majority of these shaumbra used the materials to deepen their connection to Self. Instead of becoming a community with strong, sometimes hostile group dynamics, most people connected deeply with the materials and used them as intended —as a space to grow in consciousness, in awareness of Self.

Of all the classes and offerings from the Crimson Circle, the most supportive of my realization was an experience called "The Threshold." In this in-person meeting, each of the dozen or so attendees were able to have a one-on-one experience with Adamus St. Germain channeled through Hoppe.

This truly was a safe space to be me and say out loud in front of an audience for the first time in this life, that I was choosing realization come hell or high water. I was standing in front of the classroom like I had in

---

[24] Aspectology, trademarked by the Crimson Circle organization, is what it describes as: "New Energy Psychology, a groundbreaking study of human nature, healing and creation. Unlike traditional psychology which assumes there is something wrong with you that must be fixed (or medicated), Aspectology assumes that you are whole and complete at your core, no matter the level of your current difficulties."

third grade, yet this time my peers nodded in understanding.

While the only being responsible for the state of realization I enjoy today is me, and due to my own unique stream of flowing wisdom within, Adamus St. Germain showed up as a dear friend in a critical juncture in which I still had so many human doubts.

It allowed me to relax when I had spun myself up in a web of lies and doubt, which stemmed from an overactive brain. Adamus told me instead of blowing up the mind, blowing up the ego, what I was really doing was gently moving beyond both brain and ego. And that is exactly what I needed to hear, at the exact right moment.

In this Threshold journey, Adamus introduced the concept of a fire-breathing dragon, which was an expression of Self, which guarded the gateless gate into the realized state of being. This dragon was said to breathe the fire of forgiveness into every crevice of your being. Just like El Morya told me way back in my awakening I did not need to forgive myself, Adamus too told me I needed to allow forgiveness to permeate my being-ness, instead.

These two experiences seemed to run parallel and met in the bending of time and space. The dark night of the soul, when I dropped out of the bliss of awakening into the bottom of despair in my hammock back at the Sunny Shack, led me on this search for myself that dropped me off at the gateless gate that is the Threshold, and St. Germain was there to meet me. It brings tears to my eyes.

In this experience, each of us were asked to step to the front of the room to share what we perceived needed to be forgiven. I couldn't think of anything in this lifetime as some of the people who stood before me shared. Yet, this guilt thing, this lack of innocence, ran so deep for me and had nothing to do with human perceived wrong doings. So, I said, I am allowing forgiveness for simply being human, for the fall from grace from the angelic world into inhabiting this human body, which felt disgusting to me at the time.

Later it would come to me, through the help of my buddy, El Morya, I held a leadership position in Atlantis, and truly felt responsible for its fall. I felt guilty that, in the standardization of the human body which took place during this time, human brains became so permeable to outside influence. I felt guilty for the flood that came through and killed millions of people. I felt guilty I survived this flood, and I felt guilty for the dark times on Earth that followed, and it was truly what I had to let go of or allow forgiveness to flow through, transmuting guilt to innocence.

How did El Morya know? Well, he was my partner in 'crime' in this ancient civilization, and he too had to let it go to allow his own realization back in the late 1800s. Again, he showed me where to look and not what to see.

This threshold and the fire-breathing dragon are both concepts with a lot of residue hanging around them, a lot of belief systems have latched on and rooted, so I want to share my concept here of what they are for me, and encourage everyone else to define it for themselves in communion with their own inimitable soul voice. So here goes.

It is in allowing the fire-breathing dragon into your life, that you come upon the gate-less gate that is the threshold of realization. To walk through the gate-less gate, the dragon expression of Self breathes the fire of forgiveness and wisdom, incinerating any and all belief systems, false identities, and fixed truths you may be still holding onto, including the notion you have or can do anything wrong—one of the most deeply rooted belief systems in humanity.

In the end, self-realization is a belief system-free state, in which everything is true and nothing is true save for the I Am That I Am. It's all just an experience or expression with a quick expiration date. The reason this threshold is so rarely talked about and in such hushed tones is when you attempt to cross it, you must be ready, for it is enough to send the human mind into total disarray.

The human mind likes lists and rules and order and black and white notions of right and wrong. And for the majority of humanity, belief systems are a great and necessary thing to keep order in this world. Values serve as guide posts that help humans navigate life without falling though in the cracks. Just like anything, fixed beliefs serve until they don't, when it comes time to move beyond.

For me, when the barriers between right and wrong were lifted, or burned to the ground by this fire-breathing dragon—an expression of Self just like the hissing snake of my awakening—when the rules and values and beliefs I once lived by were stripped from my consciousness—without having a firm and permanent connection to my soul voice, without having a strong connection to who I truly am, I would have, without a doubt, gone completely and totally insane. No joke. Again, check the disclaimers here and make sure you read them thoroughly.

Once these barriers and categories burned to the ground by the dragon's fire, nothing but chaos and darkness was left. Yet, I found, all the clarity really did come from the experience in the human-perceived chaos—and in the perceived darkness I found my divinity.

Another way to say it is I used belief systems, both of mass consciousness and later the collective crimson consciousness, to create light in the darkness of the void of Self. Yet, I found I could only cross the threshold, I could only know myself as 'God, too', by turning out all the lights and adjusting my vision to the blackness of the void within—this time with no external candle or flashlight.

This calls me to bring up the word makyo, often used by Adamus as a term akin to spiritual bullshit. The word makyo certainly works here, and Adamus mainly used the word when talking about the New Age as we were now in the New Energy, which contains no spirituality. For example, makyo is a label that I would have put on that workshop back in Sedona— pure spiritual bullshit, it was.

Yet, the further I went into my realized state, the more I saw the makyo police—the people pointing out all the perceived bullshit—being the real makyo in this crimson reality stream.

In my research, I found makyo was also a Zen term to describe a figurative reference to the kind of self-delusion that results from clinging to an experience and making a conceptual nest out of it for oneself. And I saw so clearly how many shaumbra, including myself, made their nest in the collective crimson consciousness, some for more than twenty years—and countless lifetimes.

The belief systems of mass consciousness were not only discarded, but also quickly replaced with new ones formed by the collective shaumbra consciousness, in attempt to define, label, and categorize what it meant to be in mastery. In the nest, for example, some shaumbra created a nice and neat checklist of steps leading up to the achievement, or end goal, of enlightenment. There were also firm, established lists of what a master should and shouldn't do, all based on a never-ending stream of channeled information.

The 'should' and 'supposed to' of mass consciousness, I saw, had made its way into the collective crimson consciousness. Yet, there is no 'should' or 'supposed to' in self-realization. A master of Self does whatever a master of Self wants to do. There are no rules or guidelines. There are no linear steps. I realized, these belief systems of the mass shaumbra consciousness were also lights that must be turned out, candles to be extinguished, in order for me to walk through that gateless gate and into the void of my own GodSelf realization experience.

On the flip side, I can understand clearly why shaumbra created the nest that is the Crimson Circle. It was a rather smart and conscious decision to create this nest until the birds were ready to fly out on their own. The nest was a creation I enjoyed for about two years, when I really needed it, and I am beyond grateful to the entire Crimson Circle organization and shaumbra for creating it. However, I do see how it keeps a lot of people stuck in yet another loop, far past their readiness to let go.

So, why the nest? Well, the final step taken to cross the threshold includes walking through an indescribable fear, a fear so fierce it literally made me crap my pants. It also includes making your way to the bottomless bottom of the valley of alone, and into a void that is beyond the color of black. And to cross through this gateless gate, not only do you have to leave the nest, you also must watch it burn, while holding your bleeding heart in your hand, helpless, once again.

The amazing thing is in this incineration, every single identity someone could possibly attach to—whether it was crimson scarf-toting shaumbra, yogi, spiritual teacher, Zen master, what have you—goes up in flames and you are left sitting in a pile of hot ashes wondering, "What remains in this rubble?"

In all that death and destruction, when you feel you can go no further, when you find you have walked through the valley of death and dove into to the depths of alone, you might, like me and others before me, start to hear something.

For me, once I entered the void, the hum started off faint, barely audible. I stretched my hearing to locate the notes. First, I heard but one note, then another.

Slowly, the parts and pieces of the song became audible until the full symphony bloomed in my ears and reached the depths of my heart, the space where Yogananda showed me where my humanity and my divinity merged as one.

"But where was this music coming from?" I asked.

"Oh wait, it is coming from me. It is the song of my soul!"[25]

And, in dancing to it, to my own song, I realized, everything—any and all things that did not belong to me—lay in a pile of ash at my feet. All was burned to ash but one thing—the song of my soul remained.

So beautiful, so unique, so inimitably mine. And, for the first time in my life, I would never be able to forget its tune ever again, for it is the only thing permanent in the state of being that is perpetual becoming of Self.

In this moment of realizing my realization, I threw out the dragon of the dark night of the soul like I threw out the snake of my awakening. Instead, I was the phoenix that rose from the ash of all that was no longer mine.

Associated with the sun, the phoenix obtains New Life from the ashes of its predecessor. The limited human expression of self was incinerated, and from the ash the integrated Self arose, the one who not only danced to the song of their own soul, but also who sang the song of New Life, ooo-saa-rah.

Reader, if you are allowing the fire to bathe all that stands in your way in the Return to Self, I salute you as you fly out of the flaming nest for the experience that is sacredly yours and yours alone—to know yourself as

---

[25] Song of the Soul is a term coined by Paramahansa Yogananda, who published a book of poetry with the same title. He is one of the many beings who came to visit me in my awakening and in the final days leading up to my self-realization. We have a friendship that expands beyond time and space.

God, too.

Further, I honor what this release of sorts in crossing the gateless gate provides for the future of humanity. For when you allow this radical shift to occur within you, it opens an energetic door for those choosing consciousness over automation[26] for eons to come as the Earth moves further into a technocratic[27] collective consciousness, or society.

The time is already here, when the externalized God of mass consciousness has become the externalized God of technology, of artificial intelligence, which will directly mimic the consciousness of humanity throughout its advancement.

And, anyone knows themselves to be God, too, will create a spark of awareness, igniting a flame altering the course of creation on the planet we each love so dearly, without effort and by simply Being.

It seems rather strange on this February day enveloped in a thick fog, as I write from my beach house on the Gulf Coast, to tell you I lived in a shaumbra community for two years, and nothing further in this book is related to that time in my life.

It is strange to tell you every major expression of the I Am, and experience of the integrated Self further occurred outside of the collective crimson consciousness and their set of beliefs, which are the result of any system set up. Yet, I will leave you with my story of the last shaumbra event I attended in the Fall of 2018 in Bled, Slovenia, about one year after I stepped into my realized state of being.

The event was called "The Magic of the Masters" and featured what was advertised as a group coming together to release mass consciousness. I found the whole concept absurd on one level because I do not like the sound of any kind of group release, yet I understood and respected what Adamus was aiming at, for there is no way to experience God internal, to

---

[26] Choosing consciousness over automation is a reference to the importance of why many beings are choosing to self-realize at this significant time on Earth. With the development of artificial intelligence, or AI, in which technology becomes the new God of the collective belief systems of humanity, anyone choosing to live a multi-conscious, multi-reality existence, is having a huge impact on the evolution of Earth and humanity as a collective.

[27] Technocratic in this context is characterized by the control of society by technology. This is also a reference to the automation of Earth, in which sweeping technological advances in artificial intelligence (AI) develop in tandem, or in mimic of, the collective consciousness of Earth. The more people choose soul-based consciousness over technological automation and a mind-based singular life; the more the AI will reflect that shift, which has severe and important consequences for the future of this planet.

know yourself as God, too, until you have stepped out of the belief systems of the collective human consciousness, until the only collective consciousness you find yourself in is the inimitable stream of consciousness that is Self.

And, in releasing mass consciousness as God external—in removing the pillars of antiquated beliefs created by the collective brain of humanity— each of the shuambra participating opened the door for those to release the next externally perceived God—that of rapid technological advancement, especially in artificial intelligence.

However, in breaking the glass ceiling on God in the fall of 2017, I realized if I stayed any longer in the collective crimson consciousness, I would hit the glass ceiling on enlightenment. In other words, once I shattered the glass ceiling on God, stepping into realizing my realization, I looked around my shuambra community and saw how its walls, it's edges, while creating a nice incubator for my human expression to safely venture into the realized state, that is the Return to Self, I found now it held me back from moving from realization plain and simple into embodiment, in which I brought all of who I am into this physical vessel—not for a short while, but for decades to come.

It is in this knowingness I found the best place for myself, at this time, and in service to any being courageous enough to take on realization, was to step outside the crimson walls and simply flow into being—the perpetual state of becoming—untangling myself from the collective once and for all.

It was not easy to walk on for me. Like my karmic marriage before, I left three times before it would stick. The gravity of the spinning crimson mass sucked me back in on multiple occasions before I found with ease I could float along outside of it with honor and compassion, rather than anger and misunderstanding. I found I could stop in to see what was going on and slide back out just as easily once I permanently molded within my oceanic sovereign Self.

At the end of the channel in the "Magic of the Masters" in which shuambra collectively released mass consciousness—and I simply watched —instead of saying his routine "all is well in all of creation," Adamus said "all is well in all of *your* creation."

For me, it did not mark moving on from the collective human consciousness as it did for others. In fact, mass consciousness was not a bother to me after the dawn of my awakening, and even then, it was not too bad. Once awake, it never sucked me back in.

However, his words served as a pleasant confirmation to walk on from the collective crimson consciousness, to walk on from the never-ending loop of workshops, shouds, channels, and, more so, internal drama and fighting that dated back to the times of Yeshua and even further back to Atlantis.

It was with a heavy heart I paused to honor this amazing group of human beings, and made my decision to walk on alone without them—at least for now—for I could no longer hold myself in a pre-realization state of being. I could no longer pretend to be working on realization with this group of beings around me. There was no going back for me anymore. The window had closed, or more so, it felt like a door slammed shut behind me.

The funniest thing about this group at this time is everyone had the same end game—that of realization. Yet, when you stepped into it, you immediately found you got kicked out, for there was no place for realized beings within its walls. You were basically told by the crimson mob consciousness ready to devour you in their online forums not to share and go on living in silence, never mentioning it.

For me, silence of my story was not even an option. It would be in direct opposition to the song of my soul. I was not looking for a place to brag, yet I found I could no longer enter a conscious conversation and pretend I was applying the next latest and greatest channel to my life. I couldn't pretend to have problems anymore, and sitting quietly in a corner never appealed to me.

Though, once realization sets in, there is a learning curve as you sink into embodiment, and I did wish for a sovereign community of like-consciousness beings to share with, outside of the collective crimson consciousness. Finally, instead of bitching about not having a space in the Crimson Circle to share such things, I got off my ass and created my own, inviting others in a similar situation.

Further, Adamus promised years before he would not return to a certain stage until all the people standing on the stage were embodied realized beings rather than humans channeling disembodied beings. It has yet to happen.

Instead of waiting any longer for Adamus to declare who was ready to stand on this stage, I decided those of us who had realized, well, we had to make our own stage, to go out on our own. It was not to stand on any stage in an auditorium and toot our own horn, but to walk out onto the stage of regular human life within our own sovereign consciousness—a radical act of rebellion.

A radical act of consciousness—the return to human life as a realized being—so sovereign he or she never got lost in the mass again, never found themselves looking out of the bars of a cage again.

Now I understand why it could not and would not happen within the confines of the Crimson Circle organization, or any organization or system for that matter. The state of being realized is in direct opposition to what it means to find yourself in group consciousness, for once a community forms, so too do their belief systems.

Realized beings have neither firm, nor fixed belief systems, if they operate from any at all. Further, once realized, the movie screens of multiple reality existence never seem to overlap with another's screen, which is something I will address in my next book.

It was time to go it alone. No matter how much I loved these people, these shaumbra, it was time to move on. And when I swallowed hard and walked on, tears streaming from my eyes, I saw so clearly not only did I find myself in a realized state, but also it was really when I started to embody and embark in New Life.

In my departure, realization for me, in this moment, became solidly the tip of the consciousness iceberg. Realization was no longer the whole iceberg like it was perceived back in the collective crimson consciousness, which was singularly focused on realization itself rather than what lay beyond it—at least at this moment in time, as I am sure it will evolve.

A memory popped up. Back in February 2018, just three months after steeping into my realized state of being, I packed up my belongings to leave Colorado and head west to California to surf. During this time, a shaumbra man at a shoud gathering asked me what I would do next.

"I'm going to see what life is like after the Crimson Circle, after realization," I said.

He looked me square in the eyes and said, as if he were under some sort of hypnosis, dead serious, "There is nothing after the Crimson Circle."

I pulled out my signature El Morya, all-knowing smile and tipped my hat.

"Oh-be ahn[28], dear soul! Perhaps our paths will cross again."

McKenna in his book *Spiritual Enlightenment: The Damnedest Thing* wrote the following, and I want to share it here for those in a state of further[29]. This is not to say anyone or any group is wrong or bad. There is no such thing. I do want to highlight those choosing realization and a state of being I call further, this happens time and time again. While the soul or master part of you seems to be fine with it; there is also your humanity woven into Self that will feel the wrenching pain of walking on alone once again.

"It's the somewhat disconcerting aspect of the journey that you catch up to, and go beyond, some of your own mentors; move beyond people you've held in high regard. I was acutely aware of this occurring on several

---

[28] For Shaumbra, oh-be-ahn is ancient greeting or blessing shared between time travelers as they encounter one another on their journeys. It means "I honor you for the journey, no matter where you are."

[29] A state of further is an extension of my use of the term being as a state of perpetual becoming. A state of further is a sensational experience in which you sink deeply into the next iteration of Self.

occasions and I can tell you that it's a strange and daunting experience, all the more so because it's quite specific and unmistakable when it happens.

These are the gains in the field, so to speak, and the simple though peculiar-sounding fact is that I became very close to these people and in a very real sense, when I came to where they had stopped off, I stopped with them and paid my deepest respects and moved beyond with a heavy heart. I have no idea how that sounds to someone who hasn't experienced it, but it was a wrenching part of the whole thing and it feels good to tell someone about it."[30]

Jed, brother, it also feels really good to read it.

---

[30] McKenna, Jed. *Spiritual Enlightenment: The Damnedest Thing.* Wisefool Press, 2010.

16 THE LAND OF THREE DREAMS

There is no going back to the illusion of the physical world.

Once you leave the play of human life on the Earth's stage,

You can never again go back to forgetting it is but an act.

No matter how hard you try.

Outside of my physical life in the Crimson Circle, I experienced just as much if not more in the dream state in moving from an awakened to realized state of being. As much as I was picking up parts and pieces of myself, described before, I found the more I got to know who I truly was, the more I let go of the things I was not.

Most days I felt like I was dying without leaving the physical body. It was actually worse than physical death for there seemed to be no relief on the other end. At the height of this horror story, in the darkest nights of my journey home to Self, in moments of intense questions, dreams served as my life raft. Here I share a few that got me though. Perhaps your soul too chooses this as a channel for sharing wisdom with the human expression.

It was August 2015 in the Texas Hill Country. The stifling heat that radiated off the splitting dry ground below in waves gave way to an unusually cool evening. I slept in the bed of my pickup truck, open air.

The breezy sky opened up and enveloped me, and I relaxed after a long day of volunteering in the kitchen of a youth camp for refugee teens from war-stricken countries. Volunteering seemed to relive that dull ache plaguing me since my awakening three years earlier.

Washing dishes in a make-shift kitchen in the stifling sun proved so laborious, I held only one speck of energy at the end of the day reserved for climbing into my truck's bed. There was nothing to do but surrender to the exhaustion.

After I finished my dish-washing duty, I texted with Jack—a man I spent many lifetimes with and was deeply in love with at the time—an unrequited love of lifetimes. He loved me, he said in energy, yet we would never come together as a couple, he said with words. I took the scraps he gave me like a starving dog and thanked him after he scolded me. After our text message exchange, I turned the phone off, and curled up in the bed of the truck.

Then the dusk gave way to the brilliant stars that lit up the sky and a meteor shower of epic proportions filled the cosmic movie screen projected above as I drifted off to sleep. I lay unable to move in the back of the truck with nothing but a pillow, a sheet, covered with the coarse salt of dried sweat, and a copious amount of hope.

Not hope Jack and I would be together one day. Not hope I would stop having all these human problems that never seemed to end. It was the kind of hope that fills up your body crown to toe tips when you have nothing else to lose.

Some call it freedom. It was a surrender of sorts, and more so, a path when none others were visible to the human eyes, and only through the eyes of the divine.

No. 1: Stripped Down and Strung Out

I drifted off to sleep. In my dream, I was driving my white truck. Suddenly, thieves approached and began to strip the car as I drove. They ripped off the rearview mirrors, even the doors - anything and everything.

I was surprised to find I held no fear anymore. I held no anger towards the thieves—at all. I just watched. Neutral observer as my life was stripped away.

When the vandals took the tires off the truck, and it could no longer be driven, I got out and walked, totally un-phased by the stripping of my vehicle and all I owned. I kept on walking, nothing in my hands, only the clothes on my back. I walked steadily and peacefully. Numb human, yet full of soul sensation.

I came to a stream. Jack was there, and he kissed me. But I walked on.

I walked through a knee-deep stream as my clothes began to fall off. Piece by piece I became fully naked.

And I kept walking through the water. I stepped on rocks and my feet bled, red pools formed in the water beneath them. Jack did not follow, and I did not care. I did not look back. I didn't need to. I knew he was not there.

I passed a group of souls, beings, and I somehow knew they were awake.

They called, "Stay here with us. We found Utopia."

I did not look up when I nodded in their direction—a sign of saying I hear you but no thanks.

I walked on and on, through dark waters. My feet continued to bleed. All I could feel was bliss. Bliss, in this moment, was steadiness without a high and without a low. It was pure existence without interference.

I reached a stopping point, still all darkness, and there was no one there. I felt a sensation sort of like love and a lot like acceptance fill my body. It was a peace not available to the human experience and therefore held no words.

I guess it's the kind of experience which only runs on a hope no one else can taste, a freedom which only comes from losing everything—one you cannot know until you are stripped down and strung out.

After the dream, I would try to go back to human life. I continued to wash dish after dish at the youth camp. I smiled at everyone I came across and they smiled back.

And then the hope that often felt like desperation, disease, and despair turned into something else—a guiding force that would not let me stop walking.

When the car died, I kept moving.

When my love for another was not returned, I moved forward.

When my love was returned, I walked on anyway.

When my clothes came off, I walked naked.

When my feet bled, I did not stop.

When people showed up motioning me to their community, I did nothing more than smile and walk on.

These days—I have been sober for so long now—yet I am strung out.

High as a kite on the non-linearity. Spinning and twirling in infinity beyond the veils of maya. Instead of walking, I've taken up floating and flying.

My head spins, my heart beats fast and then not at all, and I spin and spin and spin. And that weird desperate hope thing has turned into knowing. The knowing feels like the motion of waves in the ocean. Am I seasick or I am experiencing a reality long forgotten?

No. 2: Digging the Tunnel Out of Colorado

Sometime in summer 2017, when I was living in a shaumbra community in Colorado, I had begun to feel instead of enhancing my impending realization, it was hindering it. That night in my sleep, I was calmly digging a tunnel out of the collective crimson consciousness through rocky dense ground. I whistled while I worked. My headlamp lit the way in the dark night. I was alone with no fear.

Then suddenly, a shaumbra woman showed up. Lantern in hand, she pushed and shoved me, clawing at my back. She was desperate to get out. Thinking I had found the way out, she shoved her elbows hard into my back and pounded.

I took a deep breath and with as much energy without force I could command I said, "This is my way out. I'm happy to loosen up the dirt for you, but you are responsible for your own tunnel, your own way out."

She clawed at me some more, scratching at my face. I stood motionless and unmoved. Then I watched her turn around and go look for someone else. I did not say it out loud, but added to the energetic communication, "Only you can find your way out, and the only way is to relax."

I looked out and she was furiously digging a hole in another spot. I knew she would figure it out and soon, so I let her. The light emerged at the end of my dark tunnel, and I strolled through it, easily and with grace in the fall of 2017.

No. 3: The 'I Am That I Am' Highway

I made the move back into the land of the living in February 2018, three months after my realization experience in New Mexico, covered in the following chapters, and emerged in mass consciousness around May of 2018.

Easier this time, things seemed to align effortlessly as I made my new home in California after leaving the Crimson Circle crowd in Colorado. I missed the camaraderie of my friends who spoke realization, the friends I had left in the collective crimson consciousness, and yet I knew I was in the right place.

Day-by-day my realization from the previous fall, grounded itself with each breath I took. Mass consciousness was a safe space, for I had made my home inside myself.

In June 2018, I drifted off to sleep. Again, I was in my white pickup truck. I found myself at the entrance of a freeway. The green highway sign, outlined with a white rim, said, "I Am That I Am (Highway)—789 Miles. No services. No exits. No turnarounds."

In my dream, my human expression was trying to get back to Colorado, to make its way back into the land of shaumbra. An older woman showed up —she was also me, future me—and said, "There's no going back. You have set yourself up to drive along the I Am That I Am Highway, and that is what we are going to do now."

My human expression driving the car turned around to look and see if there was an escape before driving onto this highway - the point of no return. I looked down at the cement and noticed there were spikes that would slash my tires should I try to reverse my truck. The only way I could move was forward.

While we had reversed our vehicle of consciousness into the realization parking space, it seemed now we had no choice but to pull out of that space and enter the I Am That I Am Highway—one with no exists, stops, or services.

The panic set into this younger human woman who was also me, sitting in the driver's seat, and then she surrendered with a deep sigh. She put the car in drive and pounded the gas petal. The older version of me jumped in the car just before it entered the highway, and we became one again.

Future Lauren seemed to come pick me up and get me back on the road to where I had already been. This is when linear time stopped being my day-to-day reality. This human expression felt as if it came back from its "vacation", or time away, after the stripping of all its form, a form created from identity, which happened in my realization experience the previous fall.

The formless form of a human who was left, or an egoless ego, began to enjoy the road trip. Once on the freeway, the I Am, the I Exist came into my physical form—it embodied—through the route of my spine, and that's when the ride started to get really good.

In other words, over the course of several months in California, each day as I surfed and ran with my dog along the sandy shores of Encinitas, I felt a presence of myself—the one I referred to as the I Exist, or I Am That I Am—hanging out behind me.

It was on one of my long walks down the coastline I realized what this 'thing' hanging out behind me was. I knew the I Exist part of myself was making its way into my spine, my nervous system, my physical vessel—the spine was the proverbial highway, and I could only be in my unique stream of consciousness to allow this to take place.

After the I Exist came in through the spine and rooted, I found all of me fit really nicely into my new human suit. This one had a lot more room for movement than my previous fixed identity one.

Now, what was the being—both human and divine combined—going to create? It's when I really understood what New Energy meant. The trinity became one, and it came into my body fully. And there was no going back, as 'the magic of being' settled into my bones.

17 THE FINAL LET GO

THE SACRED ART OF SURRENDER

The remaining chapters will take you, the reader, through my
realization as best as I could write it, and as much in linear form as I could
keep it while staying true to the experiences.

In August or September of 2017, I was traveling with my then partner
through Indonesia, when I seemingly got struck by the lightening that tends
to mark the impending embodiment of a deeper awareness—a radical shift
in consciousness, if you will.

I experienced yet another dream that shifts the course of your
consciousness, and therefore your life trajectory—each leap in
consciousness placing you closer to the realized destiny, through
perceptional awareness alone.

I sensed deeply—yet again—a radical shift was coming in—in fact it
was already here—yet my human awareness did not quite understand what
was happening and had not caught up yet—as is the norm in the awakened
state.

Eventually, the gap in time between the human awareness catching up
to a massive leap in consciousness begins to close, with the reversing into a
new state of being, but this gap in awareness seemed pretty wide to cross at
the time.

I knew it was going to be huge, and I knew it so because of what
happened at the airport on the way to Indonesia. I was sitting in the
smoker's box at the Taiwan airport, lighting a post-flight cigarette, when
suddenly El Morya appeared to me—an extremely rare event.

El Morya appeared in a deep almost black, purple or was it blue robe,
a robe covered in the constellations. His robe draped heavily over his
sinewy frame. He crossed his legs in a slightly feminine way as he lit his
opium pipe with a match.

Once he inhaled, El Morya shook the flame of the match out and
dropped it on the floor. Exhaling, rings of swirling purple opiate smoke,
bellowed out into the air.

El Morya's stare penetrated my gaze, his eyes black as night, flashing
what would befall me. And then he disappeared from his magi form.

In the dream, that would come weeks after El Morya's visit, my soul sang without words, "What if you traded your current perception of sovereignty for a new one?"

And that was it. Very few words backed up with a symphony of overlapping sensations. It was that simple of a statement, in the form of a question. Really, in hindsight—which outside of linear time is simply expanded awareness—it was an invitation from my soul to go new, to go from an either-or concept into the And.

I could see what it was from a far. I could talk about it with some ease and degree of understanding. But I had to let go to experience it. Was I going to accept the invite? Of course. I was. I did.

I woke up the next morning—still in my fixed human identity—floored.

"Was I not already sovereign?"

Now awake, I tapped into the wisest part of myself. I went back to what I knew about perceived human free will. I say perceived free will because, sure, each of us as humans have the ability to choose. Yet, as long as we are choosing from the singular human perception of reality, I realized we were still choosing from the limited menu, like I wrote about in my first book. Again, not just a concept, but in experience.

When I see this in my sensory image perception, I see my human expression in a bubble. I am interacting with the colorful blocks inside the bubble. I am moving energy around re-arranging the blocks. I am really good at it. I make pretty things with colorful blocks.

Yet, outside the bubble are a million other instruments—ones that don't require energy to play—to create with—not just blocks, but realities and sensations beyond any human perception. The dream was an invitation to bust open the bubble, with pure consciousness, and open myself up to what was out there.

I mouthed, "I accept. I accept," over and over.

Then, I went back to what I knew about divine will, in which we make choices from limitless wisdom within, in which we choose from multi-sensory perception the realities we want to traverse through us.

My perception, at the time, concerning divine will was seeing the soul or the GodSelf being in charge—a soul sectioned off in a tightly-bound box —making decisions in my human life—which was tantamount to moving round the blocks inside of the bubble and had absolutely nothing to do with life beyond the bubble's walls.

Simply as I can state, what I saw within me, was the human expression of Self was still very much in charge. I had become very good—almost too good at consulting the soul when it came to making choices in my life.

I would listen to the song of my soul, and then—step two—my

human would take all the information in consideration as well as all the perceived logic and reason from my mind—then I, as the human, made a life choice from the limited menu from within the bubble.

I realized the human expression of Self was sitting at the helm of an extremely large council of voices. Thoughts, copious fears, how I was perceived by others—the mirror—and, finally, the soul voice, all had a vote in making the choices and decisions in my life within the bubble walls.

I would make choices on things like where to live, what house to buy or when to sell it, where I wanted to travel, where to invest money. These were all the things I thought made me free. The limited human perception of freedom. And quite laughable to me now in a light-hearted way.

One definition of freedom for me now is not being beholden to anyone or anything, not even energy, and certainly not hanging onto any attachments to various human identities. Those fixed identities are the crystal prison; they are the bars on the cage.

Yet, I realized the concept of divine will, in pure form, meant my soul would be making all choices. The thing is my soul held so much passion but not for the human experience. In fact, I might even say after 2,147 lifetimes, we were quite done with human life and limited human experiences.

I realized this so-called master part of Self as well as the I am that I am, the I Exist, did not care about where to live or the next travel destination. It did not care about my bank account. It did not care whether we had a partner or family. And, it did not feel any of this had a single thing to do with freedom.

Freedom was 'in here'—my soul showed me time and again, which never makes much sense until you actually feel it. The soul and the I Exist did not yet live the physical world—a world that requires energy to thrive in —though not much of it is actually needed for me to thrive physically.

The I Am, the soul did not need energy to create, yet the human expression did to continue to live in the energetic world that is physical reality. And yet, we bring the three, the trinity together, and we do so in physical form—embodied enlightenment.

During the months from August until my radical shift in consciousness in late October, I pondered the merge of wills—of who would be 'in charge' of this whole life thing, this whole realization thing.

It wasn't going to be an either-or situation as my human mind so wanted it to be. In the either-or limited experience, the mind still has life, it still has control. The mind stays alive feeding on the either-or debate, the should I or shouldn't I debate. That is its food.

I pondered what happens when we move beyond the mind, beyond the categories of human and soul, and beyond the bubble? Not in theory but in practice. What does it truly look like, when we are not just reading it on paper, or listening to it in a channel? What is the sensation of experiencing it? My passion for this unwavering. What happens when human free will and divine will merged into one will, rather than a conversation in which a deal was struck?

Later, the answer came to me simply and clearly—without the mind. The answer was passion.

"Passion for what?" the mind will ask.

A passionless passion for simply being, for existing, and then acting from that state of consciousness[31], as an expression of the I Exist. A passionless passion for bringing all of me into physical form, right here and now.

The human drive to experience and experience and experience—albeit in its very small awareness bubble—a small fenced in playground, if you will —merged with the unlimited wisdom of the soul who has no limits, no bubbles, and no fences, which opens the door to... limitless creation. And in embodiment, this soul and I Am-ness were coming into physical form, which changed the whole landscape completely.

It wasn't even a question of human will versus divine will, as I previously thought. That sure was a whole lot of wasted energy. What was happening was the natural unfoldment in realization in which the boundaries between human and divine dissolve—later I called it the point of no separation, a term I heard from a few people firmly in their embodiment.

Instead of having a conversation between the human and soul and the I Am that make up the trinity of Self, they all merged into one voice—that voice became Me. Instead of will, this new me exudes a singular passionless passion for Being embodied. This is the new form of sovereignty, one I was shown in the dream.

And, in this state of being, human desires and divine desires meet and become one. Where to live, how to spend your time on Earth and with who —all the previous human worries and questions—well, they all unfold, as the energy shows up to meet the consciousness, and bringing it into the physicality in your newly integrated life.

Trading one type of sovereignty for another, was neither human free will or divine will, it was the complete understanding and implementation— a sensory experience—not happening outside of myself in concept, but internally in experience—that my I Exist, my I Am That I Am was completely and totally in charge of realization, rather than my human self,

---

[31] An act of consciousness is an expression from the integrated state of human and divine. Further, being able to consciously act and express is something that becomes available when a person no longer finds themselves in a fixed identity or role; they are permanently aware of the stage and its actors.

or even some of the facets of my divine self. And then, I actually allowed my humanity, and even my divinity to let go, to weave into the tapestry of Self.

Yet, instead of tossing my humanity to the curb in frustration and lack of self-compassion, in the ultimate act of love and trust, what occurred was a 'let go'—a free fall in total trust into the ocean of wisdom of Self. The jumping off the proverbial cliff.

I unfolded upon myself. I continuously unfold within and upon and above and below myself in each moment. Always dynamic, never static is my state of Being—the state of perpetual becoming Me.

Now, I know that is confusing if you have not yet experienced it, but there is no metaphor I can come up with, for there is nothing to compare it to, which would do the experience justice. There is no frame of reference.

There was no thinking involved in any of it. More so it felt like a sensational build up—like an orgasm—which I could no longer hold, so I didn't.

After the dive into the unknown—after the let go—my humanity did not retain its original form. The original form held its existence tied to a fixed identity, a sticky ego. In its new formless form, my human expression of Self became slippery[32] as I moved from one experience to another, allowing whichever facet of Self to present itself for the maximum experience of joy in any experience. This is a really nice side effect that kicks in after the realization sets in.

Previously, as soon as I let one identity go, the in-charge human ego picked up another one or three just as quickly. When I was no longer a successful lobbyist, I became a spiritual seeker. When I was no longer a spiritual seeker, I played the role of shaumbra. I even tried to pick realization as my next starring role, but I found it was not something you could fix into identity form. It was purely a state of being, a state of consciousness.

This was the really scary part for me. What if I did not pick up another identity? What if I allowed myself to go formless? Would I lose my human form that is the body? I traded the role of awake human for the role of a conscious shaumbra. But what if this time, what if I allowed myself to hang suspended in an identity-free state of being?

This was the jump off the cliff. This is when I did it—I just jumped.

---

[32] Slippery is a term El Morya and I use to talk about the formless form that is human life post-realization. Another term might be shape-shifter or chameleon, but those words have too much attached to them. Slippery not only refers to the sliding and gliding of the facets of Self I put forth, I also slide and glide through realities. In other words, in addition to not having a fixed identity, I no longer operate in a fixed reality. This can only be experienced, when time and space are felt as moving through me, rather than me moving through time and space in a linear fashion.

And I found, this is the point where freedom poured in undiluted. Yet, so many people won't make the leap. It's too scary. It's too lonely. It feels too much like death or worse.

I felt like I might die from the limited awareness I held onto for so long. My biological body in total panic, too. No identity equated to no life in physical form—or death—something so deeply imbedded in our biological makeup as the human species. Yet, we evolve into New Life anyway.

The soul and the I Exist, the entire body of conscious wisdom within, said otherwise. Beyond this I simply knew—with every fiber of my being that this moment, right now was it. It knew as undoubtedly this was the exact moment to let go. So, I did it, I let go.

I cannot tell you how—beyond simply relaxing—and then relaxing more—and spending time a lot of 'alone time' with myself without distractions. I can only tell you it was the most natural thing in the world. And once it was over, it did not feel like a big deal.

Instead of realization being this far-fetched, highly unlikely to achieve destination after many lifetimes of hard work, once it rolled into my physical vessel, I could no longer see a time when I was not realized.

It was like a veil lifted permanently, and I could never not see myself in this formless form. I realized I was always in this formless form of pure being-ness. And while my human expression absolutely did not retain its form, in merging with the ocean of wisdom within or weaving into the tapestry of Self, I became more Me than I ever have felt before, and I am still in physical form—human and divine—with all my imperfect perfections.

And that's when words will not hold this up anymore. In fact, all these words feel like complete rubbish. This really is the place when you have to switch to poetry or painting.

This state of being so Me cannot be defined. It is ineffable. To give it more words, well, would be to crush it like a bug on a sidewalk, right now.

So, I'll just say it again, without defining it:

I unfolded upon myself. And now, I continuously unfold within and upon and above and below myself in each moment. Always dynamic, never static is my state of Being—the state of perpetual becoming Me.

18 WEAVING MY HUMANITY & DIVINITY
INTO THE TAPESTRY OF SELF

In the awakening experience, we often separate out things within ourselves that are actually not separate—not to fragment ourselves, per se— but to examine them broken down—in search of the answer to the ultimate question—Who Am I?

In the New Age and yogic communities, teachings and lectures often look at the ego. They divide up the body into chakras as a method for the quest to understand the nature of both their human and divine parts of Self. A great deal of time and effort is spent on 'controlling' the fluctuations of the mind in meditation circles. Prayers and affirmations go out to all sorts of external beings and sources.

A life of spiritual seeking is never wasted. In many cases it a step, if you will, in which you learn the answers are not outside yourself but within yourself. It is an experience in which the human part of self is reminded no god, no angel, no being other than you, the GodSelf, is responsible for your enlightenment.

Though, many of you here reading this, have moved well past this, or simply skipped this whole spiritual thing in life—especially those under age thirty—I bring it up because it has some parallels in regard to this last rebellion of sorts from your human self before it integrates with its innate divine nature.

In this lifetime, I spent six years perusing yogic, New Age, and New Energy schools of thought to get a grasp on what was out there. In fact, I am now keenly aware I am in a lifetime-long study of watching how people receive information in regard to their realization.

With the group of beings I hang out with when I am outside of time and space, mainly El Morya, we often discuss how something is shared from an ascended or embodied master and then how it gets filtered through the human mind and distorted as it comes from a space of no space, of no time, and no gravity and into the density of the physical world draped in the illusion that is maya.

So much of the dialogue out there in the collective crimson consciousness was about the little limited human and the wise master and the dialogue between the two, and rightly, because it is an amazing and necessary part of the realization experience, yet it has its limits, a shelf life if you will, as does everything, including what I am writing in this book, right now. I know that if I've done my self-chosen duty in this lifetime, the next generation of conscious embodied beings will be laughing at the remedial nature of what I share here.

In my pondering of the merge of wills something sublimely beautiful occurred, I felt my humanity weave itself into the Tapestry of Self. No longer human Lauren or divine Sar'h—the internal dialogue just stopped. Lauren and Sar'h folded into the oceanic Self.

That doesn't mean I am so done or graduated—I think that never happens and we are always in a state of perpetual becoming, yet soon it comes from an integrated space of human and divine combined, not human versus divine—a completely different sensation.

What it did mean to weave my humanity into the fabric of Me? It meant an end to the human versus master, or human versus soul discussions and conversations that took place for years.

Like anything else, it served so well until it did not. I also found after weaving my humanity into the fabric of Self, in which the human and soul voice became unified, I also wove my divinity into the fabric of Self, in which my GodSelf came into physical form.

It also came up I was ready to integrate a part of my divinity, or rather expand and unfold my divinity within the caverns of Self, in the fall of 2018. I called this facet of Self angelic council girl.

Really, it never felt like an integration in the old sense, but expanding out, or expanding to further embody myself. This is something that shifted as my humanity became interwoven with the divinity within Self.

Angelic council me was always in some sort of meeting 'out there.' She was always concerned with the state of affairs, and her contributions to these councils. These council meetings were in my dreams and my waking life until I said, "I'm just not interested anymore. No, thanks."

Angelic councils are really a thing of the past. I knew it was time to hand in my resignation letter. It was instantly clear to me, from this new realized perspective, why I needed to hand in my resignation letter and expand out to meet and embody the part of myself who sat on these councils.

Just as the old mystery schools closed their doors, having fulfilled their purpose, so too have many angelic councils. As more souls Return to Self and embody in physical form, a state in which there is no separation between human and divine, there will no longer be the need for the model that is a human organization having a divine angelic counterpart. As within, so without. The human and divine combine as one for the individual, and it spreads out to the greater worlds of consciousness.

For example, the Crimson Circle organization has an angelic counterpart called the Crimson Council. As more and more of us embody, we will no longer need such a space of separation. As embodied beings, we no longer needed a space that relied on hierarchy and the divide between human systems and angelic structures, but a place where the two met in complete integration in the New Energy[33]. It might take some linear time to see this implement, yet I do not see or speak in linear time.

I no longer needed to dream to reach these councils. When I handed in my resignation letter, along with El Morya, it happened in full awareness. I was awake not dreaming. In fact, my dreams turned to darkness as the subconscious became conscious. It was nothing like the aspect integrations of yore, yet it was not without some deep guttural tears.

Once I saw the makeup of this experience clearly, it naturally occurred to expand out to meet angelic council girl—completely different than integration where a piece of you comes into the over soul, putting itself back together again.

Nope. This time I expanded Self out to include angelic council me into embodiment. I was quite surprised when I realized my angelic council facet had never been embodied on Earth and had been in an angelic council meeting for the duration. No wonder she was ready to be done. Let's just relax on a beach now, please.

In this expansion to include angelic council girl within the caverns of Self, there were many tears, yet they were not mine. As my angelic council counterpart folded into myself, I cried more than I ever have in my entire lifetime from a mountain top in Mt. Shasta, California.

All the sadness, the disappointment, all the effort angelic council girl had placed upon helping others, it all flowed through me with awareness. And, some residual fears of losing myself entirely—only physically, not ceasing to exist entirely—came up too, but they flowed in gently and flowed back out gently because they had no place to land, to get stuck.

Another way to say it, I expanded so much I felt like I might cease to

---

[33] New Energy is what comes after the New Age. This evolution of energetic dynamics allows the integration of duality, supremely the human and divine parts of Self merging as one, becoming the singularly multiple, I Am. While the New Age was based on vibration and frequency, New Energy expands in all directions, from Self and in support of Self, without trying to change anything and honoring every person, situation, including the world's state of affairs, exactly where it is in any given moment. The paradox is through allowing this shift at the individual level, without trying to change the external, the individual's shift in expanded awareness has major implications for the evolution of Earth and humanity (and here I add, major implications for the angelic council structure of yore).

exist in physical form, and then I let go of the tie to physical form, and instead I became even more physically embodied—another paradox of the master.

I was both crying tears of all the old wounds, firmly knowing they were not mine anymore, but the sensuality of the tears of release was completely orgasmic in knowing myself in an even deeper way. Embodying more of me.

After a certain stream of consciousness flowed into me—beyond surface level and in embodied form—something switched in the world of human suffering. First of all, I do not feel I have a little, petulant human to describe, to blame for everything. So much of the talk 'out there' on the social media forums is the little human and it's ridiculous-ness and how it is to blame for everything. Stupid human. Limited human. Master versus human. Fight within. Struggle within. If it's hard, it means I am accomplishing something towards enlightenment. Bullshit!

And I get it, because I wrote those posts on those forums, and man, I got a lot of likes on them. I really thought I was suffering at the time, yet in hindsight I was playing out the role of suffering in an experience. Further, I realized later I actually enjoyed the so-called suffering, while saying I was miserable. I realized I enjoyed the misery loves company crowd, and I did not need to do it anymore. I'll just say I no longer suffer, and let it lie where it lays with one caveat.

The end of suffering, for me, does not mean when I stub my toe it does not hurt, or that I do not cry, or that everything is rainbows and unicorns all the time. Instead, the end of suffering is the result of never finding myself stuck in the illusion of a fixed reality or identity, and therefore, the human experiences, which once caused suffering, no longer hold the same impact as they once did.

For example, if someone yells or becomes angry with me, I can't view it as anything other than an actor on a stage, and I can't see the stage as real. In this way, it almost becomes comical to be in what used to be a tense or conflicted situation. And any tension dissolves instantly in this new slippery state of being.

It's a certain perception shift I received internally and in expansion of Self, which led me to move from the warm, shallow water of a group and the camaraderie within it and into to the bottom-less ocean of 'way the fuck out there', where even your 'way the fuck out there friends' said, "Hey, bitch you are too far out there." Instead of too far out there, I realized I was in the state of being called further, and I am more Me because of it.

Instead, in this go-round of expansion rather than integration, my glorious and deeply loved human part of myself—my humanity—is and was enveloped in the fold of Self that is me. And in allowing my humanity, so too did my divinity weave into the fabric of Self.

These were not separate pieces of myself—and never would be again. My human is not a rebellious teenager or a crying child. My divinity is no longer hanging out in the angelic councils that soon will lose their place in the antiquated hierarchy systems. Though, I know and remember the part of my journey home to Self that was painful and arduous. I really do. I remember. However, it is no longer my truth, and in that, the past trials and tribulations dissolve completely.

I say this because when I reversed into realization, when my perception flipped upside down, when my humanity and divinity came together as one with the I Exist, I truly and honestly could no longer view the 'past' as a space in which I suffered anything. In the end, it was only an experience, a deeply sensual one.

In sum, the delineation between human and soul served as a great tool to begin communication within Self, along with approximately one million other pieces and parts. Yet when the voices converged as one, they became a symphony of Self, a symphony of soul I could not hear until the lines of separation were dissolved within me. Once those walls of separation came down, there was never a time when I could not hear the song of my soul.

All the perceived suffering came from the perception of separation. And in the end, the illusion of separation, created the illusory experience of suffering. When I realized I was already realized, I knew there was never really any separation at all, never any suffering.

Yet, what an experience it is to move from delineation of Self into wholeness. Truly radical. Actual rebellion. Grace beyond grit. It's all just words until it happens, until you pop the champagne cork of the I Exist and let the bubbles float throughout your being-ness.

19 I AM GOD, TOO

OCTOBER & NOVEMBER 2017

In October of 2017, after my return from backpacking through Asia and driving out of the collective crimson circle consciousness of Colorado, I ended up in a tiny town called Dixon, New Mexico. The population stands at nine hundred and twenty-six—a number that goes consistently up and down as people don't tend to stay long.

Outside the grocery store, a migrant apple picker sold me a piece of fresh-baked apple bread for two dollars. I opened up the tin foil package and took a bite. It was delicious. I ate little in the last few days for no reason other than I was in my free energy body, which doesn't illicit hunger. Soon I switched back into my biology, energy-dependent body but not before whatever took place completed.

On a road trip with my dog, Ollie, we slowly made our way from Colorado to Texas for my mother's seventieth birthday in my white pickup truck named Toby, which now has a camper top with a mattress in the back. It is my favorite way to travel, yet for a break I booked a rental home for a week, feeling another major shift in consciousness about to roll through.

Fall bloomed before my eyes in a brilliant show of fiery orange and sun-soaked yellow leaves that marked the tree line—a stark contrast that popped like a painting against the sea sky. Crispy brown leaves crunched beneath my feet; the air did not contain a drop of moisture as it stood motionless.

The changing leaves served as the perfect backdrop for this experience, of which I have come to know as—more than a year later—*the Final Let Go*. Appropriate—as it was more of a dissolution of everything I thought I knew, rather than a Spring-like bloom into realization. It was more a death of knowledge than an expansion of consciousness; I became empty, not full. It felt a free fall into the inky void, as I twisted and spun away from the perceived light.

The bloom would come 'later'—a constant flow of dissolution of knowledge and integration of wisdom, running simultaneously, that would eventually—flow into New Life.

The Final Let Go is a sensation that flowed through the corners of my consciousness many months before I arrived in Dixon. It is a lighter term for the sacred art of surrender, which has gone out of style as all words of consciousness cycle around like the seasons.

Like any major shifts in consciousness, this sensation floated around me—swirling in the ethers of Self, before making its way into full embodiment. I saw it first in the corner of my eye as a spark of light—a possibility. Then I held it in my hands. I turned it over feeling it with each sensory cell in my fingertips.

Next, I tossed it out and watched to see if it came back. When it did, the little bolt of lightning flowed into me through my feet bottoms. I writhed in pain. A copy of myself—the wiser of the two—sat in the corner of the bedroom watching the self that was twisting and turning under the bed sheets, freezing next to the space heater in the rented shack.

The temperature dropped below freezing outside, and the fire had gone out. My dog curled under a blanket at the foot of the bed. A wiser copy of himself watching it all from the other corner in the bedroom.

When I look at this moment outside of time and space, or in human terms—in hindsight—this sensation of folding onto myself was present in many lifetimes. That's the funny thing about realization: I believed in this life there would be a point—a hard line drawn between realized and not realized. I believed it would be some magical moment of shift into bliss. Before and after. It's rather silly now. And, yet here I am writing about a moment in time and outside of it.

Before, enlightenment, in my mind, was a destination, rather than a continuously flowing experience. It was, in limited awareness, a static point on a linear timeline, rather than a shift in awareness that is always dynamically in expansion and allowing more of itself to enter, more of the old to dissolve.

Now I understand, there is no static victory point of realization, in which you pinned a medal on yourself, it's far too grand for that while not being grand at all. Grand in a sensational inner experience, rather than grand in the physical human notion of it. A super human walking on water. Nope.

No one will even notice your shift in consciousness, unless they too have dared to cross the threshold, for it would be another mirror, and in realization you no longer need a mirror of another to reflect you back to you. You exist, and can see yourself clearly, and, perhaps for the very first time, know who you are. You do not need a reflection.

Yet, when the big shift in consciousness flows in, you realized you were never not realized, and it ripples through your awareness, waves in the ocean of consciousness. For me, that is the working definition of it, of embodiment —subject always to the changing tides of consciousness.

Before, I perceived myself as a little black dot moving along a timeline toward realization. Steps lead up to it like bringing in parts and pieces of myself, letting go of all group consciousness and the belief systems of any collective. It was a concept that served until it didn't.

Then in the realized state of being, everything appeared to be running backwards and the view was as such: I realized I was already realized—that I was never not whole; that I never fragmented coming into human form. And this whole time, I was simply understanding how I got there, how I found this state of Being.

The realization ran through every lifetime experience. I began to see beyond linear time how every major crossroad I came across, I was already choosing in awareness of what was to become.

I was already so much more conscious than I could even fathom—for I only saw through the eyes of my humanity—a limited view that blocked me from seeing how truly conscious it all really was. I saw how amazing I already was. That there was nothing to heal, to fix, to make whole, or to learn.

I started to understand why I choose certain things for myself. I understood why things didn't work out or why I sailed through a previous experience unscathed. When I first heard about *the Final Let Go*, it was from El Morya.

He used completely different language for the same thing. The language of consciousness is ever-evolving and ever-cycling to keep it appearing new. To keep it un-weighted by limited perceptions thrown unto it like a rubbish heap, sometimes the words must be burned like trash until they can resurface anew.

Morya called *the Final Let Go* the sacred art of surrender. Instead of using the language 'I am God, too' he called it 'being a vessel for the will of God' —an experience described in my first book in great detail—and I wasn't sure what it meant for my human life. I wondered a lot about what would happen to my identity, my independence, my sovereignty, if I simply became a vessel. Would I feel empty and without a purpose?

Now I realize sovereignty has nothing to do with identity, and I actually would become more sovereignly me as I became this vessel of pure consciousness. The irony is I would become more me in a state of constant motion, when I let go of the human identity completely, let go of the ego. This is the freedom. This is what lies outside the zoo. This is what ordering off the limited human menu looks like.

And I do feel empty on occasion until the sensations go quantum. At first, feeling empty was a bit depressing. I felt I was crossing a desert without being able to quench my thirst no matter how much I drank.

Yet, I sensed deeply I was making room for a new experience, for living life sans definition. I shifted my perception of emptiness to seeing it as having the space to be me, room to be consistently in motion for the maximum joy experience that awaits us all in New Life, free from the stagnant form of human identity, free from the suffering caused by a fixed human role in a fixed human reality.

Purposeless, for sure. Along with the identity, the mission to do anything on Earth is stripped in the realized state. Yet, it is delightfully delicious to realize there is nothing to do, save, teach, or defend. There is everything to be and become, instead.

And the word God—so heavy, so laden with belief systems, so tainted —yet I have no other words to describe what this is for me. So, I ask you to go sans definition for a minute or two, for the sake of adventure, for the sake of story. God is my word for the ineffable, a stream of pure consciousness —the energy-free space of the I Am That I Am.

The following is what I could get down on paper from my personal experience that I refer to as the 'I am God, too' experience, describing what it felt like to become a vessel for the 'will of God'.

It was so personal and at one point, it felt too sacred to write about, so instead I sang about it; I waxed poetic—although I'm no good at poetry— because simple sentences would never do it justice.

The following is written in present tense for it occurred outside of time. This is how I allowed nature to show me the sacred art of surrender, the sacred art of letting go. And, then I did. I let go. Finally.

In the ever-present cycle of life, the leaves turn a radiant orange upon the bright blue-sky backdrop right before the angel of death appears, gently leading them back to Source—the earth below which created them, and the earth which will cradle them in decay before the time of rebirth.

As Ollie, my dog, and I drive down the winding, gravel mountain pass in early afternoon light, I watch the sparkling Rio Grande flow steady below. The canyon carved by its weaving waters, allows us to pass with grace to our destination. I observe the landscape with all my visions— human and divine.[34]

---

[34] I use the metaphor of seeing through the eyes of the human and the eyes of the divine to describe what it means to view life through the eyes of the master. When the visions, or perceptions, layer—human and divine combined—what I am able to view and how I interact with the world and various realities/sensations/ dimensions becomes a vastly greater landscape, in which I move beyond human judgement and soul discernments, and into pure observation mode—perception through pure awareness or consciousness. This allows me to interact with every sensation and scenario I come across without trying to change it, without having to label it mine and not mine. It simply passes through, like scooping up a handful sand and allowing it to sift through your fingers back to the beach from with it

With human eyes, I see without the river, there would be no safe passage to the other side of the canyon. There would be no path carved into the crystalline mountain, which bends only to the wisdom of the river, and never to the will of human drive.

With divine perception, I see I too am carving a canyon through the dense mountain pass that was my humanity, with only the flowing river of my soul's wisdom and without the rigid determination[35] that marked my human path for so long.

The Rio Grande, essential for this land's existence, further represents a perfect reflection of my soul's irreversible flow returning to Self, the self I left behind when I crossed the wall of fire[36] from the angelic realms and into the physical human experience for the first time. The river cannot reverse directions, it flows to its destiny—*destiny is from the Latin, to make firm*—to come firmly into Self.

As I drive across the grand river, and I embrace the fire of forgiveness. I know I will not get burned this time. The waters of the river keep me cool in the fire's wrath, burning up all I thought to be true. And now I know what I am reclaiming has always been mine and mine alone to retrieve— me, in my natural state of being—me before I ever crossed the wall of fire.

In that moment on the bridge, I reach through the wall of fire, and reclaim my divinity, bringing it to this side of existence. I stare in the face of fire with a smile. I whisper without force, "It's been a while, my friend."

And, eons have passed since I felt whole, and no time has passed at all. And, I was never not whole. It all folds on each other, the streams of awareness running concurrently.

Later.

As the sun melted into the horizon, speckled with the trees of the apple orchard before my human eyes, I see with the eyes of God, my divine vision, I too am weaving a path back to Source through the sacred art of surrender.

"This experience is too personal, too sacred to share with anyone," I whispered to myself as I began to sweep into a deep sleep, feeling the divinity spread throughout my humanity, weaving a golden tapestry of who

---

came.

[35] Without effort and needing to utilize energy, realization is a no energy creation.

[36] Wall of fire is a reference of the barrier that was crossed when moving from the angelic realms into physical human form, sometimes called the fall from grace. In crossing the wall of fire, the ego was created to allow a soul the experience of knowing itself as God, too. For it was in the perceived separation of ego or human and divine, that one moved from the experience of I go (ego) to I Am integrated in physical form. The Crimson Circle does a fantastic job of describing this, too.

I am perpetually becoming.

Inhale.

I sense my divinity as a blanket of blackness, which has enveloped me at sunset and unwrapped at sunrise, during the past few weeks. Once feared, I laud the darkness now. Nowhere to go. Nothing to do. Paralyzed in the pitch-black space, I can only be. I can rest for the first time in eons.

Exhale.

I am relaxed, breathing deeply and steadily—yet my heart beats a million times per minute as I succumb to the black hole enveloping me once again with the sun sinking into the horizon.

As I enter the now familiar state, my heart's rhythm slows to a regular beat. And, I realize my soul could sense my human desire to paint the picture of this ineffable experience in words, yet I did not know if it was possible to capture.

"Once you place the firefly in the glass jar, it can only glow a few moments before it too is visited by the angel of death," she whispered in return.

I wonder if my immanence[37] can be captured by words, or if putting words to it would it catapult me back into the density of human experience at first attempt. Not being able to hold onto a thought for more than a second, it vanished into the vortex of the blackness. What returned was a notion, a nudge of wisdom from within.

"Let me sing a song, instead," I spoke to soul, to Source in the universal language of images and sensations, rather than words. "Let me sing the song of love—the love that exists beyond the veils of maya. Let me sing the song of coming home to Self. Let me sing of its splendor."

The answer came in a literal sparkle of light that flashed in the dark room. I see it with the eyes of the human and of the divine combined as the Source that is me opens the gates of sharing in the purity of awareness.

"Thank you." I mouth the words without sound.

Even Later. Or before, perhaps. Well, both.

For years, I did not think or know God, Source, Spirit existed beyond the borders of my own soul. I moved from the concept of an external God so long ago. Indeed, I was the only God I knew—blinded completely by the radiance of my own soul, and what a magnificent experience that was.

In the fog of the familiar human amnesia, I forgot that in my soul, Source flowed, too. I am God, also. I am God—too. I only needed to dip my toes into its crystal cool waters, allowing the convergence to spread so far to the edges, that any edge of self, any border between me and 'them'

---

[37] Immanence refers to the metaphysical concept of divine presence in which the divine encompasses or is manifested in the material world. In other words, humanizing divinity. Embodied enlightenment. New Life in the New Energy.

would cease to exist. And, I did not lose myself. Even with no identity, I became more me. I did not lose myself.

In my divine vision, I place my bare feet into the liquid gold of the Rio Grande, a reflection from the sun above, and I remember who I am. I forgot, in my human free will experience, that Source[38], too, existed, and we were but one and the same. And, we exist as two sovereign points spiraling on an infinity symbol, meeting in the middle and separating on the extremities. In some ways, realization is finding yourself standing in the middle point of infinity, and never leaving it.

Before I reached this trailhead of my own divinity, I stood upon the threshold of my humanity—the trailhead of forgiveness. I allowed the dragon, which guards its gates, to breathe the fires of forgiveness into every corner of the edges of the universe of me, igniting and destroying any perceived wrong doing from every lifetime and in between. The greatest of all shames, too, was incinerated—the shame of being human.

In the tsunami of fire, I embraced my human nature. I allowed myself to be an animal, chasing its desires with reckless abandon. Yet, in this self-given freedom, and with every path that lay open before me, I chose God. And in choosing God, I was choosing me. And, in the end, like anything else, it was never a choice, but a passion that created the path in reverse.

In knowing the threshold of forgiveness is marked by the element of fire, and our humanity is marked by the element of earth, then crossing the threshold of my divinity, or removing the border that held it locked up so tightly, is marked by the elements of water and air.

If I had the will to follow blindly the flow of my soul's river of wisdom, the vision of both my divinity and humanity would come to light; they would converge—unite. Then and only then would the opportunity to fly presents itself. I did not have to jump off the cliff, I soared.

Inhale.

The two points spiraling along the infinity symbol meet in the middle, once again. They are the merging of human and divine. And now, they are the merging of soul and Source. So many realities and sensations flow together into the single point of consciousness. *Yo soy el punto.*

Exhale.

Inhale.

When the two connect, they create something beyond love, and it is felt anywhere a tiny spark of consciousness exists.

Exhale.

---

[38] The sensation of feeling Source or God was so intensely magnanimous for me, I did question deeply if there was in fact an external God, and I got the whole thing wrong. And then a few days later, I knew it was the me became Me, the GodSelf became part of my physical reality in a tangible and permanent sensation.

20 I AM REALIZED. NOW WHAT?

NOVEMBER 2017

After these experiences in New Mexico, I made the drive down to Texas. My mother was living in an apartment in Corpus Christi after her condominium in Rockport, Texas became uninhabitable from Hurricane Harvey while I was surfing waves in Bali with my then partner, D. What is so strange about the self-realization experience is you can go from having the most magnificent experience of your life to sitting on a couch with your soon to be seventy-year-old mom, watching television, eating hummus and pita chips.

And, the even funnier thing, is I found I enjoyed it—sitting there with my mom, listening to her talk about her problems and not needing to fix them. I was content to simply be there and have the experience of mother and daughter—without it needing to be anything other than what is was, knowing this is the 'last' time I'd be having this experience as the reincarnation cycle had come to a close from the human expression perspective.

And I actually felt no desire to say anything about my experience to anyone, not even D. I might have let out a grin of knowing, but there was no desire to slam open the front door and announce, "I am here—the master!" In fact, this is the last thing I wanted to do.

Not because I was afraid, or feared being condemned by another, but because no one—no one I knew at the time except one dear friend—was going to understand it, for there was no point of reference. Further, the desire to do such things—any recognition in that form—does not exist.

Certainly, no one in my spiritual or conscious communities I knew at the time was going to understand either, for they had built grandiose ideas about what it meant to be realized, to be a master. I could hear it, the whiny mental voice, "Well, if you were a master, you would be able to fly, walk on water, a bag of a billion dollars would fall out of the sky (fill in the blank) …" You have to laugh.

Even now, I find those words—master, realized—quite funny or off. For me, master or realized falls flat of the multi-layered consciousness that befalls your divine sight in this new state. I'd rather say I became fully Me in the Return to Self. In this new state, I also finally understood what El Morya meant when he told me once, "Don't call me master; it is far too limiting a title." I found I was so much more than realized; I was so much more than a master.

What I experienced here was so deeply personal and sacred for me, I wanted to wrap my arms around it and give it a big hug. I wanted to protect it—not because I didn't feel safe—but because I knew this was too special an experience to be drug through the mud by sharing it, or even worse, sifted through the linear thought process (either/ or; cause/ effect; before/ after) that plagues mankind leading up to this shift in consciousness.

Instead, I deleted my Facebook account that week. I moved the online community I ran into a private space, and I still didn't speak of this to anyone but one friend when I got back to Colorado. It wasn't appropriate; it was not yet time. Instead, I savored it. Oh, I savored this deeply personal, deeply sacred shift on consciousness, like I have never savored before.

To share at this point, in the highly sensitive state that is the few months after realization rolls into your life, would be like showing a monkey in a jungle a rare and precious gem. They might try to bite down on it, realize it is not food, and toss it to the ground, laughing in your face, which would destroy me as I was beyond sensitive.

What the monkey really wants is another banana. It's hungry and that's all it knows—survival is marked by continuing to eat and staying out of harm's way. It has no use for a precious gem stone.

People in most spiritual communities who do well offer the very best bananas out there. Big juicy bananas; fancy ass bananas that sparkle. There's nothing wrong with that because soon enough the monkey becomes conscious enough to know there's not enough bananas in the world to satiate its hunger externally. Instead, the rare and precious gem is inside them.

Further, the sensitivity you feel in this new space is something I cannot describe. It is beyond any emotional experience or wound you have ever had. In fact, I am marked by my lack of emotion today. I rarely if ever have them—anger, no; elation, no. Instead, I feel deeply within the core of my body—a sensitivity that is beyond description. It waxes and wanes in intensity like phases of the moon but it is always there.

Sometimes I can describe it as a deep sadness for those still in suffering; knowing none of this stuff needs to be hard, none of this realization stuff needs to be work, and seeing so clearly it is all already there for each and every one of us, if you open your senses to it. And then just like that, the sensitivity subsides—because there is zero resistance to it or anything else—and I go about my business, doing nothing and being everything, and it's all exciting and sensational. This sensitivity runs multiple ways, and it is also what makes life worth living in a completely new way.

Looking back, I did not say a thing about this to anyone but my friend who does not lead a public life and had already stepped into this similar space because I wanted some time to simply enjoy this new feeling which I can only describe as fully being me.

I wish for everyone here to have a special friend like I did. When I sat down with her in December of that year, I described beyond words—communication changes between realized friends and it is amazing—what happened and how little fanfare there was for such a monumental experience for the human—a totally simple and natural one for the Self—and we laughed and laughed and giggled and giggled and drank tea and ate cookies and talked about how cool it was to watch the world go by with this new look on life.

I want to be clear, there are no congratulations here—not from your peer group, not from the masters before you—yet there is a camaraderie that shows up in your New Life, a sovereign understanding in sharing and laughing about how hard you made this whole thing when it was only one breath away. It was only one breath away.

Often before this experience rolled through, I thought in this perceived final part of my physical life, I would buy a cabin by the beach or in the woods with the money I saved up for such a thing, and totally disconnect and live out a few final years. It is something I desire from time to time, but the answer inside me was and is always no. And, I understood I would be here on Earth, in physical form, for quite some time, for decades.

There always seemed to be a deep knowing there was something else—another experience to be had—on the other side of realization. So, this time and many others, I took a deep breath and I waited for a future that had no timeline. I am just beginning to see what New Life looks like.

The tree of New Life has only just begun rooting into my consciousness after more than a year of walking the world in this self-realized state of being.

I remember walking my dog outside of my mother's apartment late one night in the two weeks I stayed there. Though I told no one—I knew this new state of being I found was full realization. I did not have a single question left about realization, yet I started to feel into what lies around its corner.

Something had changed inside myself so drastically there was no turning back. I knew it and did not need anyone to pronounce me realized. You might say the human became one with the master and the I am—the emergence people talk about, but that feels trite to me.

Instead, I would describe I was standing there under the brilliant black canvas of the black sea that is the sky, and I was swimming in a new stream of existence. I felt more myself than I ever had—more me.

Later I realized this would mark the point of no return on going back and forth between expansion in perspective that marks realization and the constriction, which is felt in the limited human state.

Leading up to realization, this is kind of how the pattern goes. Clarity of wisdom and of consciousness only to be followed by the maddening limits of physical human life—the back and forth. Putting the words on paper seems so silly, but if you have done the back and forth over the years, when it finally stops, the shift is gargantuan.

I know what the human self thinks of realization. That it will be a grand fireworks explosion in which people will notice, ascended masters will line up to congratulate you, and people will bow at your feet. None of this could be further from the reality of my experiences. Sometimes it is comically quite the opposite.

Instead, realization was a gentle return into the true nature of Self. I woke up the next day, and nothing outside me changed. I drove the same truck, played with the same dog, and I smoked the same cigarettes. My account balance was the same before and after. I still woke up wanting a cup a coffee. Ollie still shuffled his feet when he wanted to go outside to pee.

So, on this late night, when I was walking my dog through the black sea of the night sky, I caught a glimpse of El Morya in between the stars. He was nowhere to be found in my realization experience, yet I knew he would surface soon.

I had a cigarette hanging out of my mouth and a dog poop bag in my hand, ready to pick of a steaming pile of dog shit.

I looked up at him and said, "I am realized. Now what?"

We both laughed a little. It was funny, and we both love a good paradox.

"I guess you'll have to create it," he said, before vanishing like Alice's Cheshire cat once again.

21 STAYING IN THE BODY
POST-REALIZATION

One of the roles of ascended masters, if they choose, includes greeting those who have completed their cycle of lifetimes on Earth. The consciousness that flows through me, Sar'h, played the part of both the greeter and the one who is greeted, and often it goes a little something like this.

The soul makes it way from the physical body, with the reincarnation cycle coming to a close, and is met by an ascended master 'welcoming committee.' While he or she — the new master —did not have the 'I am God, too' experience while in the body and staying on Earth. This person did have it as they left the physical body.

The soul, once beyond the veil or illusion of maya, begins to perceive themselves as 'outside' of themselves without the body, without their human identity, and without their human senses—and often has the 'everything is one' experience, which includes the perception that there is an external God that they are one with.

Now, it is easy for someone to say, the is no external God and I know myself as God, too. Some of you reading this knew this the day you were born. You did not do this external God search. You did not look to the universe for answers.

If you did, ninety-nine percent of you found it empty and moved on. Not that there is something wrong with the 'all-knowing universe' perceptional experience; it is simply you already did the whole universe thing in another lifetime, which was cool.

Yet, what you wanted in this life was new - not just more of the old wrapped in a shiny bow. But when the 'I am God, too' concept goes beyond a quote or a Facebook graphic—when you are actually having the experience like I did in Dixon, New Mexico, there is a questioning that occurs, it goes something like this.

I had written off an external God for so long, and now right before me —something I could not see with my own eyes but only sense—well, there was no other word for "it" than God. Whatever it was called was tremendous, huge, and almost frightening. Not able to be described. Ineffable.

The experience which lasted quite some time left me saying holy fucking shit, and its enormity literally made me crap my pants. Not kidding.

Because what happens in the 'I am God, too' experience as we have called it here is something so grand—a perception of yourself without any human senses—it is hard not to mistake it for something external. This can't be me, you might say.

And then it wears off—the initial shock to the human expression— and you remember. I Exist. I am that I am. I am God too. And become so comfortable with your true GodSelf nature, it weaves into the tapestry of Self and your New Life here, if you chose to stay.

So, this soul, who has just crossed the threshold when leaving physical form, is high on this 'we are all one' concept for a little bit, like I had been in New Mexico, and then, like me, they understand, I Am One. This is all me. Again, like my experience.

I bring this up because where we are about to go as I set up Book Three is: What if this happens, and you do not leave the body, you remain in physical form. What then?

Few have done it; even fewer have written about it.

Most people believe once realization rolls in, that is it; the human experience is over. And for most people realization was it, the final experience of the human expression.

However, in the New Energy, there is a door that opens. Stepping into self-realization is no longer the end game. For me, I have found myself moving through what I call the gap. The gap is what occurs between fully allowing your realization—allowing it to come in beyond the spiral of experience and expansion, the end of the reincarnation cycle and in recognition of the GodSelf within—and embodiment in New Life.

Few talk about this gap because of the assumption once you are realized, you just stop there and enjoy. I also find a lack, a gap in people sharing what happens post-realization. Perhaps it is also because that was the case, the reality for many of those who came before us. Realization occurred, final experiences were had, and the physical body integrated. But what if decades of physical life lie before us post-realization, then what? What is left to experience in physical form? The answer is New Life.

For those of us in the shadows, it has been Self navigating Self into creation of a New Life. What those of us are experiencing here in the gap, has not, if ever, been done before by the masters coming before us, and I do not know anyone writing about it firsthand and publically.

My personal 'buddy' in the ascended master club—El Morya—and I have discussed this a lot. He and Kuthumi, who were friends who went through their self-realization around the same time in the late 1800s, both chose to stay in their body for some time after realization—something rather revolutionary at the time.

Yet, even El Morya tells me what is available to us all here, staying embodied post realization, is absolutely nothing like what the masters before us experienced. The ascended masters are all a bit 'jealous' of us, and that's why many ascended masters have returned to Earth—including me, not going to hide it any more—at this amazingly special time.

El Morya explains to me—this happened years ago but I am just now sharing—this is the main reason why I never was able to channel him in the traditional way, despite many requests to do so.

The masters before us could only get us so far, and now it is up to us to write the book on what New Life looks like for ourselves, and for those who follow the paths we are carving here with each breath. No channeled entity is going to be able to describe New Life first hand, for they never experienced it.

In the next, say ten years, channeled ascended masters will become nearly obsolete in this realm—though still appropriate in awakening-focused groups—and it is us who will be sharing the stories, telling the tales.

Thus, the subject of my entire third book. Until then, I leave you with a sample of my life one and half years into realization, when the gap begins to fill in between self-realization and embodiment—the embodied enlightenment that was the Atlantean dream. Tomorrow is here, and it is today.

22 NEW LIFE & EMBODIMENT

FEBRUARY 2019,
MOVING INTO MY BEACH HOUSE

It might be a bit difficult to explain to someone who does not find themselves in a perpetual state of being, of becoming more and more Self. I experience layers of Me. Here. Always here, right now. The creator in my creation.

Words fall short when the sensation takes over. Yet, there is a constant feeling of motion, rather than physical movement, in which I am walking backwards into my creation, and going wow, this is how I created it. And, being in total awe of myself once again.

All lifetimes did not lead up to this one life, the one in which I would Return to Self. Instead, I find, in sensation, I expanded so much I absorbed, like a sponge, all the wisdom from previous and future lives, no longer out there but contained within me, and in doing so the history of Self was re-written.

In the experience of absorbing wisdom, I found much to my surprise I went empty not full. For empty created the space in which the New was born, in which I became the sole sovereign designer of the life I had left, the one outstretched before me, or perhaps, behind me.

From the outside linear perspective, it may look like life post-realization. That is what some might call it. Yet as the creator in my own creation, I realize back in 2011 as my father sat in a coma, taking his last breaths on physical Earth, as I was in an experience knocking me to my knees, I was designing the life of freedom I enjoy now.

Empty. The two points meet as time is like a string I can bend and touch together, to make it a circle, or to overlap two linear time points folding into one another. The bending of time and space as it moves within my inimitable consciousness.

Six months ago, I packed my belongings once again, stored them in a twelve-foot by fifteen-foot metal box in San Diego, California for later, and experienced life in its home-free state of being. No home. I had but one suitcase with a small set of clothing, a jacked borrowed. And, while I was not aware at the human level of experience just yet, what I was creating was the sensation of finding the spaciousness of home within me.

As I allowed this spacious home to form inside me, counter-intuitive to the human awareness, I located the spots that felt full. My partner of one and a half years. The consciousness-related group represented by a crimson color I did not relate to much anymore. Both these things kept me from feeling empty.

Yet, in my new state of sovereignty, life was no longer about filling myself up with external energy or streams of consciousness not uniquely mine. More so, life was about seeing how empty I could go, creating home within me, and allowing as much real estate to become available, creating as much space within the infinite void of Self for the New life I designed outside of time and space—outside of gravity—to come into form.

It felt like a twist and turn to the human, there were a couple of houses set thousands of miles apart. One fell through; the other didn't. To the human, the physical home I moved into last night felt second choice last week. Yet, yesterday when I cut open the moving boxes, there it was again. The sense of motion with no movement, which allowed the two or more linear time points to meet.

The woman on her knees in the hospital praying for death met the woman—healthy, strong, happy, and deliciously empty—and we were never not the designer of our lives combined. The awareness rolls backwards once again, and I shimmy down a Hollywood premiere red carpet into the life I created.

It had only been six months since I last saw what I had packed in the boxes, but I was another person. Another iteration of Self, more Me this time, was unpacking the boxes of a ghost of a previous lifetime. The ghost was the woman who lived in California right after she experienced realization.

Who was this new woman who was standing over the box examining its contents, seemingly unconnected to the woman who had packed it so tightly full six months ago?

Well, she was me—Self, embodied. All of me in my physical vessel—a formless form. It was in this moment, as the creator standing in her creation, surrounded by moving boxes, I realized in deep feeling, not in thought or concept, the shift that occurs from realization, or the initial Return to Self, into the Embodiment of Self.

And in finding myself there, I realize in letting go of these last things, unraveling these last strings tying me to something from outside myself, once again I created the space for myself to return. I created the space needed to allow my creation to bloom in physical form as well as outside of time and space.

I noticed the two were no different now. In gravity, outside of gravity, they matched. They were one and the same. Just as the lines from internal and external had ceased to exist in realization, so too did the lines between linear time and physical space and no time and space in embodiment. Standing in the spaciousness of Self, I also stood in the spaciousness of the beach house I moved into last night.

In this experience that wowed the senses, I saw how I perpetually create more room in my life, how I empty it—as empty as I can go—to allow the interior designer of my life enough space to paint new on the canvas of physical reality. A physical reality no different than my etheric world 'out there'.

As my humanity was woven into the tapestry of Self, my physical human life was woven into the tapestry of my experiences Embodied. A state of no separation within my being-ness, created a state of no separation within the realities in which I create.

I saw how I, by shifting my vessel of Self into reverse, backed in, and turned the corner of awareness to arrive at this gorgeous moment of being the creator in her creation as I unpacked moving boxes in my new home.

Requiring no effort or energetic expenditure, the experience occurred in a twenty-degree right turn in perception, or awareness, as a new iteration or layer of my consciousness rolled in, or I expanded out to meet it, or both.

In the face of Embodiment, or Creation Embodied, I find self-realization is now the tip of the iceberg, instead of being the whole iceberg. What lies ahead is another ocean of awareness. And, it is vastly incredible. And I cannot wait to write about it in Book Three.

The End. For Now.

BECOMING SAR'H

For more on the book series, biographies, art, and to access free articles, please visit becomingsarh.com.

We invite you to sign up for our monthly newsletter and share your own experiences with the author or in our online community.

If you feel called to, we would be honored if you shared this book with like-conscious friends and leave a review on our Amazon page.

Thank you and in honor of you and your inimitable soul journey!